THE
BAY PSALM BOOK

Being a *Facsimile* Reprint
of the

First Edition, Printed by STEPHEN DAYE
At Cambridge, in New England
in 1640

APPLEWOOD BOOKS
Carlisle, Massachusetts

The Bay Psalm Book was originally published
in 1640 by Stephen Daye.

Thank you for purchasing an Applewood
book. Applewood reprints America's lively
classics—books from the past that are still
of interest to modern readers. For a free
copy of our current catalog, write to:

Applewood Books
P.O. Box 27
Carlisle, MA 01741

ISBN 978-1-55709-097-3

Introduction

THE first edition of the Bay Psalm Book, or New England version of the Psalms, printed by Stephen Daye at Cambridge, Massachusetts, in 1640, has the distinction of being the first book printed in English America.

When the Pilgrims landed at Plymouth in 1620, and founded the first permanent colony in New England, they brought with them Henry Ainsworth's version of the Psalms in prose and metre, with the printed tunes.[1] This version was used in the church at Plymouth until 1692. Elsewhere, the Puritan colonists of the Massachusetts Bay, coming over in 1629 and 1630, sang the words and tunes of Sternhold and Hopkins's Psalms, which for many years had been published with the ordinary editions of the English Bible.[2]

---

[1] The first edition of Ainsworth's version has the following title : — *The Book of Psalmes: Englished both in prose and metre. With annotations, opening the words and sentences, by conference with other scriptures. By H. A.* [With the music.] *Amsterdam: Giles Thorp,* 1612. 348 pp. 4°. (British Museum.) Reprinted in metre in 1618 (Lenox), in metre in 1642 (Prince collection in Boston Public Library), in prose and metre in 1644 (British Museum, Lenox), in metre in 1644 (Trinity College at Cambridge), and probably later.

[2] The Geneva Bible of 1569 was probably the first to have this version bound with it. The usual title is : — *The Whole Booke of Psalmes: collected into English meeter by T. Sternhold, J. Hopkins, and others . . . with apt notes to sing them withall.* More than two hundred editions between the years 1569 and 1640 are described in the British Museum Catalogue, and it was printed and appears to have been in use as late as 1841.

[v]

Introduction

The translation by Sternhold and Hopkins, however, was not acceptable to many of the nonconformists. Some of the extremists in England even called it "Hopkins his Jigges" and "Genevah Jiggs." Cotton Mather in his *Magnalia* sets forth the opinion held of it by the Puritans of the Bay Colony in the following words : — "Tho' they blessed God for the Religious Endeavours of them who translated the Psalms into the Meetre usually annex'd at the End of the Bible, yet they beheld in the Translation so many Detractions from, Additions to, and Variations of, not only the Text, but the very Sense of the Psalmist, that it was an Offence unto them."

The desire for a translation which would express more exactly the meaning of the original Hebrew led to the undertaking of a new version, not long after the year 1636, in which "the chief Divines in the Country, took each of them a Portion to be Translated." Just what portions were done by each one of the "thirty pious and learned Ministers" then in New England, or how many others aided in the work, we have no means to determine. It is related by John Josselyn,[1] that when he visited Boston on July 11th, 1638, he delivered to Mr. Cotton the Teacher of Boston church, "from Mr. Francis Quarles the poet, the Translation of the 16, 25, 51, 88, 113, and 137. Psalms into English Meeter, for his approbation." It is possible that some of these contributions of Mr. Quarles were incorporated in the new version.

The principal part of the work, we are told, was committed to Mr. Richard Mather, minister of the church in Dorchester, who probably wrote the preface also,[2] and to Mr. Thomas Welde and Mr. John Eliot, associate ministers of the church in Roxbury. "These, like the rest," says Cotton Mather, "were of so different a Genius for

---

[1] *Account of Two Voyages to New England* (London, 1674), pp. 19, 20.

[2] A rough manuscript draft of the preface, in Richard Mather's handwriting, is among the Prince MSS. in the Boston Public Library.

Introduction

their Poetry, that Mr. Shepard of Cambridge, on the Occasion addressed them to this Purpose.

> " *You* Roxb'ry *Poets, keep clear of the Crime,*
> *Of missing to give us very good Rhime.*
> *And you of* Dorchester, *your Verses lengthen,*
> *But with the Texts own Words, you will them strengthen.*"

It is unnecessary to repeat here the criticisms of Professor Tyler and others on the " hopelessly unpoetical character " of this version. Dr. William Everett aptly remarks that the fault lay largely in the excess of reverence for the subject; and he calls attention to the fact that John Milton attempted to turn nine of the Psalms into English verse, adhering as closely as possible to the original, with a result as harsh and dry as anything in the Bay Psalm book.[1]

In the meantime a printing press had been brought over to Massachusetts, while the new Psalm Book was preparing. It was mainly through the efforts of the Rev. Joseph or Josse Glover, formerly rector of Sutton, in Surrey, that this was accomplished. He raised funds in England and in Holland, contributed largely himself, procured the press, types, and paper, and engaged the printer, Stephen Daye, under contract dated June 7, 1638. Sailing with their respective families, and with three men servants to help the printer, the party arrived in New England, probably in September, 1638; excepting, however, Mr. Glover, who " fell sick of a feaver and dyed," either on the voyage or just before they started.

In March, 1639, according to Winthrop, the printing house was begun at Cambridge, the first things printed being the *Freeman's Oath*, probably on a single sheet, and an *Almanack* made for New England by Mr. William Peirce, mariner. Neither of these publications is known to be extant.

---

[1] Memorial Exercises at Newton, *Eliot Anniversary*, 1646-1896 (Newton, 1896), p. 75.

Introduction

The next thing printed was the *Psalmes* newly turned into metre, which was finished at the press in 1640, in an edition of seventeen hundred copies. It thus " had the Honour," according to Thomas Prince, " of being the *First Book* Printed in NORTH AMERICA."

From a deposition made by Stephen Daye in 1655, in the suit brought by Glover's heirs against Henry Dunster, president of Harvard College, we learn that the cost of printing the seventeen hundred copies was £33, that one hundred and sixteen reams of paper were used, valued at £29, that the book was sold at twenty pence per copy, and that the total receipts from sales were estimated at £141 13s. 4d., leaving a profit of £79 13s. 4d.

The new Psalm Book was adopted at once by nearly every congregation in the Colony of Massachusetts Bay, and for that reason it came to be known as the " Bay " Psalm Book. A revised and enlarged edition, under the title of *The Psalms Hymns and Spiritual Songs of the Old and New Testament*, was printed at Cambridge in 1651, in an edition of two thousand copies, and in this form it ran through many editions in New England, the latest being " The Twenty-seventh Edition," printed at Boston in 1762.

The churches of Salem and Ipswich did not formally adopt the new Psalm Book until 1667, in which year the Salem church decided that " the Bay psalm book should be made use of together with Ainsworth's." In Plymouth Colony the use of Ainsworth was continued as before until 1692, when the church there also agreed " to sing the psalms now used in our neighbor churches in the Bay."

Even in England, as Thomas Prince remarks, the book was " by some eminent Congregations prefer'd to all Others in their Publick Worship." Reprinted there first in 1647, and in the revised form in 1652, it ran through more than twenty English editions, the latest bearing the date of 1754. In Scotland, too, at a later period, the book was used in the Presbyterian churches to some extent, half a dozen Scotch editions appearing between the years 1732 and 1759. These English and Scotch editions were usually bound with Bibles of octavo size, and in that form many of them were imported for use in New England.

After being used for upwards of a century, and running through more than fifty editions, the Bay Psalm Book gave way to the newer versions of Tate and Brady and of Isaac Watts. Among others, the church in Dedham voted for the change in 1751; the New North Church in Boston, in 1755; the church in Ipswich, before 1757; the First Church in Roxbury, in 1758; and the First Church in Boston, in 1761. In 1755, the Rev. Thomas Prince, minister of the Old South Church in Boston, began a new revision of the Bay Psalm Book, which was finished by him and adopted by his congregation in 1757, the book being published in 1758, and in a second edition in 1773. But in 1786 the Old South Church followed in the way of the others, and gave up Mr. Prince's Revision for Watts's Psalms and Hymns.

Ten copies of the first edition of the Bay Psalm Book are known to be extant. Five of these copies were at one time in the possession of Rev. Thomas Prince, as part of his "New England Library," and by him were bequeathed in 1758, with his other books, to the Old South Church in Boston, "to be kept and remain in their Public Library for ever." After remaining in the steeple chamber of the church for nearly one hundred years,[1] three of these Psalm Books, between the years 1850 and 1860, passed into the hands of Mr. Edward A. Crowninshield of Boston, Nathaniel B. Shurtleff, M.D., of Boston, and Mr. George Livermore of Cambridge. According to a memorandum made by Dr. Justin Winsor, in August, 1871, for knowl-

[1] See *Catalogue of the Library of Rev. Thomas Prince* (Boston, 1846), pp. 10, 19, 41 (2 copies), and 104, for brief entries of the five copies.

Introduction

edge of which I am indebted to Mr. Edmund M. Barton, librarian of the American Antiquarian Society at Worcester, the volumes were transferred to these gentlemen by the late Lt. Governor Samuel T. Armstrong, who had joint custody of the Prince Library as one of the deacons of the Old South Church. " He surrendered the copies to these private hands in consideration of certain modern books given to said library, and of the modern binding bestowed on one or more of the copies now remaining in said Prince Library." The record of the ten copies is as follows : —

(1) JOHN CARTER BROWN LIBRARY, Providence, R. I. Perfect, but with a small portion of the blank margin of the title-page and the lower blank margin of the leaf of errata cut out; in the original old calf binding, re-backed. Size of leaf, six inches and seven-eighths by four inches and one-half. It was first owned by Richard Mather, one of the translators, whose autograph signature is in several places on the fly leaves and covers. From the Mather family it passed to the Rev. Thomas Prince, the bookplate of whose "New England Library" is pasted on the back of the title. By Prince it was bequeathed to the Old South Church, in his will dated October 2, 1758, "and from that time till 1860, the book remained in the custody of the deacons and pastors of that church. In that year it was given by the church, through the proper agents, to the late Nathaniel Bradstreet Shurtleff, M.D." On Dr. Shurtleff's death his library was offered for sale at auction by Leonard & Co., Boston, November 30 to December 2, 1875, but the Psalm Book was withdrawn because the deacons of the Old South Church obtained an injunction to prevent its sale. After a hearing before the Supreme Judicial Court of Massachusetts, the injunction was dissolved and the book adjudged to belong to Dr. Shurtleff's estate. It was therefore advertised again, in a four-page circular, to be sold at auction, on October 12, 1876, by Joseph Leonard; and it was sold for $1025, to Mr. Sidney S.

Rider of Providence, from whom it was bought by Mr. Caleb Fiske Harris. After the death of Mr. Harris, who was drowned in October, 1881, his collection was placed for sale in Mr. Rider's hands, and he sold the Psalm Books of 1640 and 1647 to the Brown Library, $1500 being given for them together with books worth considerable more. See *Catalogue of the Library of Dr. N. B. Shurtleff* (1875,) no. 1356; *Catalogue of Books relating to North and South America in the Library of the late John Carter Brown*, part 2 (1882), pp. 201–202; Victor H. Paltsits in the *Literary Collector*, December, 1901, p. 70.

(2) MRS. ALICE GWYNNE VANDERBILT, New York. Perfect. It is one of the five copies bequeathed by Thomas Prince in 1758 to the Old South Church, from whose collection it passed by exchange, between the years 1850 and 1860, to Mr. Edward A. Crowninshield, as related above. In the catalogue of Mr. Crowninshield's library, announced to be sold at auction by Leonard & Co., Boston, in November, 1859, the book is described as "in the original old vellum binding." The whole library, however, was withdrawn and sold at private sale for $10,000 to Mr. Henry Stevens, who took it to London, where the Psalm Book was offered to the British Museum for £150. Its purchase not being approved, the book was withdrawn by Mr. Stevens, and after being rebound by F. Bedford in "dark brown crushed levant morocco," was sold in 1868 to Mr. George Brinley of Hartford, for 150 guineas. At the Brinley sale in March, 1879, it was bought for the late Mr. Cornelius Vanderbilt for $1200. The statements in the *Memorial History of Boston*, vol. 1 (1880), and in the Catalogue of the John Carter Brown Library, part 2 (1882), that this copy was destroyed in a warehouse fire in New York, not long after its purchase by Mr. Vanderbilt, are both incorrect. Mrs. Vanderbilt writes that the book now belongs to her, and that it has never been injured in any fire. See *Catalogue*

Introduction

*of the Valuable Private Library of the late Edward A.
Crowninshield* (1859), no. 878; Brinley *Catalogue*, part 1
(1878, sold 1879), no. 847; Stevens, *Recollections of Mr.
James Lenox* (1886), pp. 61–63.

(3) MR. ALFRED T. WHITE, Brooklyn, N. Y. In
the original old calf binding, with remnants of the brass
clasps; lacking nineteen leaves, *i. e.*, title, O_2 and O_3, and
sheets W, X, Y, and Ll; and showing marks of usage.
Size of leaf, six inches and fifteen-sixteenths by four
inches and three-sixteenths. This also was one of the five
copies bequeathed by Mr. Prince to the Old South Church
in Boston, from the custody of which it was obtained
about the year 1850, by Mr. George Livermore of Cambridge, whose signature is on the inside of the front cover.
In 1855 Mr. Henry Stevens of London made a trade
with Mr. Livermore by which he received from him
twelve leaves out of this volume (sheets W, X, and Y)
to supply an imperfection in the copy which he sold afterwards to Mr. Lenox. After Mr. Livermore's death in
1865, some of his books were deposited in the library of
Harvard College, but they were subsequently withdrawn,
and all were sold at auction by Charles F. Libbie & Co.,
Boston, November 20–23, 1894, when the Psalm Book
was bought for its present owner for $425. See *Catalogue
of the Valuable Private Library of the late George Livermore,
Esq.* (1894), no. 531. See also Stevens's *Recollections of
Mr. James Lenox* (1886), pp. 61–62, where an error is
made in stating that only four leaves were taken from this
copy to perfect the Lenox copy. The same error is
repeated in Mr. Littlefield's *Early Boston Booksellers* (1900),
pp. 18–21, where another error is made about the *Souldiers
Pocket Bible*, which was not received from Mr. Stevens
as part payment for the twelve leaves, but was given to
Mr. Livermore by Mr. Crowninshield, whose inscription
to that effect is in the volume.

(4) and (5) PRINCE COLLECTION, Boston Public Library.
Both slightly imperfect, and both in modern binding. These

Introduction

are the two remaining copies of the five originally given by
Thomas Prince to the Old South Church in Boston. In
1866 they were deposited with the rest of the collection in
the Boston Public Library. They are described in the printed
catalogue as follows: "There are in the Prince library
two copies of this rare book, one of which (21. 15) is complete, with the exception of a slight mutilation of the 'Finis'
leaf, and the absence of the following leaf, which contains
on the *recto* a list of ' 'Faults escaped in printing.' The
other (21. 14) which alone has the book-plate of the 'New
England Library,' has a small part of page Ee supplied in
manuscript, and is otherwise complete." See *Catalogue of
the American Portion of the Library of the Rev. Thomas Prince*
(1868), p. 16; and *The Prince Library, A Catalogue of the
Collection of Books and Manuscripts* (1870), p. 7.

(6) HARVARD COLLEGE LIBRARY, Cambridge, Mass.
Imperfect, lacking the first six leaves and the last four leaves;
re-bound in October, 1900. The book was given to Har-
vard College Library in October, 1764, by Middlecott
Cooke, of Boston, a graduate of the Class of 1723. See
Catalogue of the Library of Harvard University, vol. 2
(1830), p. 679; and information from Mr. William C.
Lane, the librarian.

(7) AMERICAN ANTIQUARIAN SOCIETY, Worcester, Mass.
Imperfect, lacking the title-page and the leaf of errata at the
end; in the "original vellum binding." "The upper portion
of next to last leaf is torn and a corner from the first page
of the Preface." It was given to the American Antiquarian
Society by Isaiah Thomas, whose book-plate is in the volume. On one of the fly leaves Mr. Thomas has written
the following note: "After advertising for another copy
of this book, and making enquiry in many places in New
England, &c. I was not able to obtain or even to hear of
another. This copy is therefore invaluable, and must be
preserved with the greatest care. It is in the original binding.
I. T. Sept. 28th, 1820." See *Catalogue of Books in the
Library of the American Antiquarian Society* (1837), p. 43 of

Introduction

letter P; and information from Mr. Edmund M. Barton, the librarian.

(8) LENOX COLLECTION, New York Public Library. Slightly imperfect, the upper corner of leaf G being torn off, taking away portions of three lines on both sides; in modern binding. Size of leaf, seven inches and one-sixteenth by four inches and three-quarters. This copy turned up at the sale of the *Fourth and concluding portion of the extensive and valuable collection of books, formed by the late Mr. William Pickering, of Piccadilly, bookseller,* at Sotheby & Wilkinson's auction rooms, London, on Jan. 12, 1855, in a lot which was catalogued as follows : —

> 432 Psalms. The Psalms of David, 1640 — Another copy, 1639 — The Psalms of David, translated by Bishop King, *russia, gilt edges,* 1654 — The Psalms, by Barton, 1654 — Another copy, 1682 — The whole Book of Psalms, with the Singing Notes, 1688 — The Psalms of David, in Meeter, 1693 12mo. 8 vol.

The lot was bought by Mr. Henry Stevens for £2 18*s.* On examining the book, Mr. Stevens discovered that twelve leaves (sheets W, X, and Y) were lacking, having been left out by the original binder. These twelve leaves were finally obtained from Mr. Livermore's copy, as related above, and after being mended and re-margined, they were inserted in this copy; the book was rebound in red morocco by F. Bedford, and was then sold by Mr. Stevens to Mr. Lenox for £80. See Stevens, *Recollections of Mr. James Lenox* (1886), pp. 57–62, where, besides the error in stating the wrong number of leaves found lacking in this copy, an error is also made in referring to the wrong number in the Pickering sale catalogue (" 531 Psalmes. Other editions, 1630 to 1675, black letter, a parcel "), which was bought by " Holmes " for nineteen shillings.

(9) MR. E. DWIGHT CHURCH, Brooklyn, N. Y. In the original old calf binding; lacking the first four and the

last three leaves, which were supplied later in facsimile.
Size of leaf, seven inches (nearly) by four inches and five-
eighths. Accompanying the book is a manuscript note of
which the following is an extract: "It belonged to the
Shuttleworth family, & is now handed to my daughter
Sophia S. Simpson, to be used at her own discretion, by her
beloved mother. Sarah Shuttleworth, 1844." About the
year 1872 it was bought by the late T. O. H. P. Burnham,
of the "Antique Bookstore" in Boston, not knowing at
the time exactly what it was. Years afterwards, on com-
parison by Mr. R. C. Lichtenstein with the 1640 edition
in the Public Library, it was found to be a genuine copy
of that edition. In August, 1892, it was sold to the late
Bishop John F. Hurst, of Washington, D. C., and in
February, 1903, shortly before his death, it was bought by
Messrs. Dodd, Mead & Co., from whom it passed to the
present owner.

(10) BODLEIAN LIBRARY, Oxford. "The copy in the
Bodleian is perfect. It formerly belonged to Bishop
Tanner." — Cotton's *Editions of the Bible* (1852), p. 177.
Bishop Tanner died December 14, 1735; and by his will,
dated November 22, 1733, he bequeathed his manuscripts
and books to the Bodleian. "Unfortunately, when Tanner
was removing his books from Norwich to Oxford, in December, 1731, by some accident in their transit (which was
made by river) they fell into the water, and were submerged
for twenty hours. The effects of this soaking are only
too evident upon very many of them. The whole of the
printed books were uniformly bound in dark green calf,
apparently about fifty years ago; the binder's work was
well done, but unhappily all the fly-leaves, many of which
would doubtless have afforded something of interest, with
regard to the books and their former possessors, were removed." — Macray's *Annals of the Bodleian Library* (1868),
pp. 155–156. See the *Caxton Celebration Catalogue* (1877),
p. 165; Stevens's *Bibles in the Caxton Exhibition* (1878),
p. 117.

Introduction

In October, 1860, it was announced in the *Historical Magazine* that C. B. Richardson & Co. " have nearly ready a *fac-simile* reprint " of the Bay Psalm Book, limited to fifty copies ; and in the November number it was stated that the whole edition had been taken up by subscribers. The book appeared fifteen months later, with title as below, and with a preface by Dr. Shurtleff, dated January, 1862, in which we are informed that all the peculiarities of the original, including broken type, inverted letters, and other errors, had been reproduced exactly by the modern compositor :

A Literal Reprint of the Bay Psalm Book Being the Earliest New England Version of the Psalms and the First Book Printed in America (Fifty Copies for Subscribers) Cambridge Printed [at the Riverside Press] for Charles B. Richardson New York 1862 vii pp., psalms (148) leaves, list of subscribers (2) pp.   8°.

Besides the fifty copies for subscribers, Mr. Livermore had fifteen extra copies printed on thick paper for presentation, besides five copies on India paper, and one copy on vellum.   The vellum copy was retained by Mr. Livermore, at whose sale in 1894 it brought $76.

In issuing the present reproduction, which is the first one ever made in exact facsimile, the publishers have used the copy belonging to Mr. Church, and also the copy in the Lenox Branch of the New York Public Library.   In comparing these two copies of the original edition side by side, it was found that the printed matter on every page of the Lenox copy measured a little more each way than in the Church copy, the variation being nearly one eighth of an inch. The difference in size, however, was not typographical, but was caused merely by the shrinkage of the paper, which in one copy had been more exposed to the air than in the other, and was not so smooth and flat.   The peculiarity referred to will be noticed in comparing the first three leaves of the preface, reproduced from the Lenox copy in the

Introduction

present facsimile, with the three leaves following, reproduced from the Church copy. In each case the facsimiles
are the exact size of the originals. It is an interesting fact
to know that shrinkage of paper can make such a difference
in the measurement of the printed page in different copies
of the same book.

WILBERFORCE EAMES.

New York, October, 1903.

THE
VVHOLE
BOOKE OF PSALMES
Faithfully
TRANSLATED *into* ENGLISH
Metre.

Whereunto is prefixed a difcourfe de-
claring not only the lawfullnes, but alfo
the neceffity of the heavenly Ordinance
of finging Scripture Pfalmes in
the Churches of
God.

Coll. III.

*Let the word of God dwell plenteoufly in
you, in all wifdome, teaching and exhort-
ing one another in Pfalmes, Himnes, and
fpirituall Songs, finging to the Lord with
grace in your hearts.*

Iames v.

*If any be afflicted, let him pray, and if
any be merry let him fing pfalmes.*

Imprinted
1640

The Preface.

THe finging of Pfalmes, though it breath forth
nothing but holy. harmony, and melody : yet
fuch is the fubtilty of the enemie, and the enmity
of our nature againft the Lord, & his wayes, that
our hearts can finde matter of difcord in this harmony, and crotchets of divifion in this holy melody. for- There have been three queftiõs efpecially ftirtïg côcerning finging. Firft, what pfalmes
are to be fung in churches? whether Davids and o-
ther fcripture pfalmes, or the pfalmes invented by
the gifts of godly men in every age of the church.
Secondly, if fcripture pfalmes, whether in their
owne words, or in fuch meter as englifh poetry is
wont to run in? Thirdly· by whom are they to be
fung? whether by the whole churches together
with their voices? or by one man finging alõe and
the reft joynïg in filéce, & in the clofe fayïg amen.
    Touching the firft, certainly the finging of Da-
vids pfalmes was an acceptable worfhip of God,
not only in his owne, but in fucceeding times. as
in Solomons time 2 *Chron*. 5. 13. in Iehofa-
phats time 2 *chron*. 20. 21. & in Ezra his
time *Ezra* 3. 10, 11. and the text is evident
in Hezekiahs time they are commanded to
fing praife in the words of David and Afaph,
2 *chron*. 29, 30. which one place may ferve
to refolve two of the queftions (the firft and the
laft) at once. for this commandement was it ceri-

moniall

moniall or morall? some things in it indeed were
cerimoniall, as their musicall instruments &c
but what cerimony was there in singing prayse
with the words of David and Asaph? what if David was a type of Christ, was Asaph also? was
every thing of David typicall? are his words
(which are of morall, universall, and perpetuall
authority in all nations and ages) are they typicall? what type can be imagined in making use
of his songs to prayse the Lord? If they were typicall because the cerimony of musicall instruments was joyned with them, then their prayers
were also typicall, because they had that ceremo-
ny of incense admixt with them: but wee know
that prayer then was a morall duty, notwithstand-
ing the incense; and soe singing those psalmes not
withstanding their musicall instruments. Beside,
that which was typicall (as that they were sung
with musicall instruments, by the twenty-foure
orders of Priests and Levites. *1 chron 2 5. 9.*) must
have the morall and spirituall accomplishment in
the new Testament, in all the Churches of the
Saints principally, who are made kings & priests
Reu. 1. 6. and are the first fruits unto God. *Reu.14
4.* as the Levites were *Num. 3. 45.* with hearts &
lippes, in stead of musicall instruments, to prayse
the Lord; who are set forth (as some iudiciously
thinke) *Reu.4. 4.* by twenty foure Elders, in the ripe
age of the Church, *Gal.4. 1,2,3.* answering to the
twenty foure orders of Priests and Levites
1.chron. 25. 9.   Therefore not. some select
members

members, but the whole Church is commaund-
ed to teach one another in all the severall sorts
of Davids psalmes, some being called by himselfe
מִזְמוֹרִים : psalms, some תְּהִלִּים Hymns
some שִׁירִים : spirituall songs. soe that if the
singing Davids psalmes be a morall duty & ther-
fore perpetuall; then wee under the new Testamēt
are bound to sing them as well as they under the
old: and if wee are expresly commanded to sing
Psalmes, Hymnes, and spirituall songs, then either
wee must sing Davids psalmes, or else may affirm
they are not spirituall songs: which being penned
by an extraordiary gift of the Spirit, for the sake
especially of Gods spirituall Israell, not to be
read and preached only (as other parts of holy
writ) but to be sung also, they are therefore most
spirituall, and still to be sung of all the Israell of
God: and verily as their sin is exceeding great,
who will allow Davids psalmes (as other scriptures) to be read in churches (which is one end)
but not to be preached also,(which is another end
soe their sin is crying before God, who will allow them to be read and preached, but seeke to
deprive the Lord of the glory of the third end of
them, which is to sing them in christian churches.
obj. 1 If it be sayd that the Saints in the primitive Church did compile spirituall songs of their
owne inditing, and sing them before the Church.
1Cor. 14, 15, 16.
Ans. We answer first, that those Saints compiled
these spirituall songs by the extraordinary gifts of

* 3
the

the spirit (common in those dayes) whereby they
were inabled to praise the Lord in strange tongues, wherin learned *Paræus* proves those psalmes
were uttered, in his Commēt on that place *vers* 14
which extraordinary gifts, if they were still in the
Churches, wee should allow them the like liberty
now. Secondly, suppose those psalmes were sung
by an ordinary gift (which wee suppose cannot be
evicted) doth it therefore follow that they did
not, & that we ought not to sing Davids psalmes
must the ordinary gifts of a private man quench
the spirit still speaking to us by the extraordin
ary gifts of his servant David? there is not the
least foot-step of example, or precept, or colour
reason for such a bold practise.

obj. 2. Ministers are allowed to pray conceived
prayers, and why not to sing conceived psalmes ?
must wee not sing in the spirit as well as pray in
the spirit ?

Ans. First because every good minister hath not
a gift of spirituall poetry to compose extempora-
ry psalmes as he hath of prayer. Secondly. Suppose he had, yet seeing psalmes are to be sung by a
joynt consent and harmony of all the Church in
heart and voyce (as wee shall prove) this cannot
be done except he that composeth a psalme, bring
eth into the Church set formes of psalmes of his
owne invētion; for which wee finde no warrant or
president in any ordinary officers of the Church
throughout the sciptures. Thirdly. Because
the booke of psalmes is so compleat a System of
psalmes

pſalmes, which the Holy-Ghoſt himſelfe in infinite wiſdome hath made to ſuit all the conditions,
neceſſityes, temptations, affections, &c. of men
in all ages; (as moſt of all our interpreters on the
pſalmes have fully and perticularly cleared)there
fore by this the Lord ſeemeth to ſtoppe all mens
mouths and mindes ordinarily to compile or
ſing any other pſalmes (under colour that the
ocaſions and conditions of the Church are new)
&c. for the publick uſe of the Church, ſeing, let
our condition be what it will, the Lord himſelfe
hath ſupplyed us with farre better; and therefore
in Hezekiahs time, though doubtleſſe there were
among them thoſe which had extraoridnary gifts
to compile new ſongs on thoſe new ocaſions, as
Iſaiah and Micah &c. yet wee read that they are
commanded to ſing in the words of David and
Aſaph, which were ordinarily to be uſed in the
publick worſhip of God: and wee doubt not but
thoſe that are wiſe will eaſily ſee; that thoſe
ſet formes of pſalmes of Gods owne appoynt-
ment not of mans conceived gift or humane
impoſition were ſung in the Spirit by thoſe holy Levites, as well as their prayers were in
the ſpirit which themſelves conceived, the
Lord not then binding them therin to any
ſet formes ; and ſhall ſet formes of pſalmes
appoynted of God not be ſung in the ſpirit now,
which others did then ?

Queſton. But why may not one cōpoſe a pſalme
& ſing it alone with a loud voice & the reſt joyne
with

with him in filence and in the end fay Amen,

Ans. If fuch a practife was found in the Church of Corinth, when any had a pfalme fuggefted by an extraordinary gift; yet in finging ordinary pfalmes the whole Church is to ioyne together in heart and voyce to prayfe the Lord. -for-

Firft. Davids pfalmes as hath beene fhewed, were fung in heart and voyce together by the twenty foure orders of the muficians of the Temple, who typed out the twenty foure Elders all the members efpecially of chriftian Churches *Reu* 5. 8. who are made Kings and Priefts to God to prayfe him as they did: for if there were any other order of finging Chorifters befide the body of the people to fucceed thofe, the Lord would doubtleffe have given direction in the gofpell for their quallification, election, maintainance &c. as he did for the muficians of the Temple, and as his faithfullnes hath done for all other church officers in the new Teftament.

Secondly. Others befide the Levites (the chiefe Singers) in the Iewifh Church did alfo fing the Lords fongs; elfe why are they commanded frequently to fing: as in pf. 100, 1, 2, 3. pf. 95, 1, 2, 3. pf. 102. title. with vers 18. & *Ex.* 15. 1. not only Mofes but all Ifraell fang that fong, they fpake faying (as it is in the *orig.*) all as well as Mofes, the women alfo as well as the men. v. 20 21. and *deut.* 32. (whereto fome thinke, Iohn had reference as well as to *Ex.* 15. 1. when he brings in the proteftant Churches getting the victory over the

Beaſt

Beaſt with harps in their hands and ſinging the
ſong of Moſes. *Reu.* 15. 3.) this ſong Moſes is
commanded not only to put it into their hearts
but into their mouths alſo: *deut.* 31. 19. which
argues, they were with their mouths to ſing it together as well as with their hearts.
Thirdly. Iſaiah foretells in the dayes of the new-
Teſtament that Gods watchmen and deſolate
loſt ſoules, (ſignified by waſt places) ſhould with
their voices ſing together, Iſa. 52. 8, 9. and *Reu.*
7. 9, 10. the ſong of the Lamb was by many together, and the Apoſtle expreſly commands the
ſinging of Pſalmes, Himnes, &c not to any ſe-
lect chriſtians, but to the whole Church Eph. 5. 19
coll. 3. 16. Paule & Silas ſang together in private
Acts. 16. 25. and muſt the publick heare óly one
man ſing? to all theſe wee may adde the practiſe
of the primitive Churches; the teſtimony of ancient and holy *Baſil* is in ſtead of many *Epiſt.* 63
When one of us (ſaith he) hath begun a pſalme,
the reſt of us ſet in to ſing with him, all of us with
one heart and one voyce; and this ſaith he is the
common practiſe of the Churches in Egypt,
Lybia, Thebes, Paleſtina, Syria and thoſe that
dwell on Euphrates, and generally every where,
where ſinging of pſalmes is of any account. To
the ſame purpoſe alſo *Euſebius* gives witnes.
Ecclſ. Hiſt. lib. 2. *cap.* 17. The objections made
againſt this doe moſt of them plead againſt joyn-
ing to ſing in heart as well as in voyce, as that by
this meanes others out of the Church will ſing

as alfo that wee are not alway in a fuitable eftate
to the matter fung, & likewife that all cannot fing
with underftanding ; fhall not therefore all that
have underftanding ioyne in heart and voyce to‑
gether ? are not all the creatures in heaven, earth,
feas : men, beafts, fifhes, foules &c. commanded
to praife the Lord, and yet none of thefe but
men, and godly men too , can doe it with
fpirituall underftanding ?

As for the fcruple that fome take at the tranf‑
latiõ of the book of pfalmes into meeter, becaufe
Davids pfalmes were fung in his owne words
without meeter : wee anfwer‑ Firft. There are
many verfes together in feveral pfalmes of David
which run in rithmes (as thofe that know the heb‑
rew and as Buxtorf fhews *Thefau.* pa. 02,.) which
fhews at leaft the lawfullnes of finging pfalmes in
englifh rithmes .

Secondly. The pfalmes are penned in fuch
verfes as are futable to the poetry of the hebrew
language , and not in the common ftyle of fuch
other bookes of the old Teftament as are not
poeticall ; now no proteftant doubteth but that
all the bookes of the fcripture fhould by Gods
ordinance be extant in the mother tongue o' each
nation, that they may be underftood of all, hence
the pfalmes are to be tranflated into our eng‑
lifh tongue; and if in our englifh tongue wee are
to fing them, then as all our englifh fongs (accord
ing to the courfe of our englifh poetry) do run in
metre, foe ought Davids pfalmes to be tranflated
into

into meeter, that foe wee may fing the Lords
fongs, as in our englifh tongue foe in fuch verfes
as are familar to an englifh eare which are com-
monly metricall : and as it can be no juft offence
to any good confcience, to fing Davids hebrew
fongs in englifh words, foe neither to fing his
poeticall verfes in englifh poeticall metre : men
might as well ftumble at firging the hebrew
pfalmes in our englifh tunes (and not in the hebrew tunes) as at finging them in englifh meeter,
(which are our verfes) and not in fuch verfes as
are generally ufed by David according to the poetry of the hebrew language : but the truth is, as
the Lord hath hid from us the hebrew tunes, leſt
wee fhould think our felves bound to imitate
them; foe alfo the courfe and frame (for the moſt
part) of their hebrew poetry, that wee might not
think our felves bound to imitate that, but that
every nation without fcruple might follow as the
grave fort of tunes of their owne country fongs,
foe the graver fort of verfes of their owne country poetry.

    Neither let any think, that for the meetre
fake wee have taken liberty or poeticall licence
to depart from the true and proper fence of
Davids words in the hebrew verfes, noe; but it
hath beene one part of our religious care and
faithfull indeavour, to keepe clofe to the
originall text.

    As for other obiections taken from the diffi-
culty of *Ainfworths* tunes, and the corruptions in

our common pfalme books, wee hope they are
anfwered in this new edition of pfalmes which
wee here prefent to God and his Churches. For
although wee have caufe to bleffe God in many
refpects for the religious indeavours of the
tranflaters of the pfalmes into meetre ufually an-
nexed to our Bibles, yet it is not unknowne to
the godly learned that they have rather prefented
a paraphrafe then the words of David tranflated according to the rule 2 *chron.* 29. 30. and
that their addition to the words, detractions from
the words are not feldome and rare, but very fre-
quent and many times needles, (which we fup-
pofe would not be approved of if the pfalmes
were fo tranflated into profe) and that their
variations of the fenfe, and alterations of the
facred text too frequently, may iuftly minifter
matter of offence to them that are able to com -
pare the tranflation with the text; of which fail-
ings, fome iudicious have oft complained,
others have been grieved, wherupon it hath bin
generally defired, that as wee doe inioye other,
foe (if it were the Lords will) wee might inioye
this ordinance alfo in its native purity: wee have
therefore done our indeavour to make a plaine
and familiar tranflation of the pfalmes and words
of David into englifh metre, and have not foe
much as prefumed to paraphrafe to give the fenfe
of his meaning in other words; we have therefore
attended heerin as our chief guide the originall,
fhūning all additions, except fuch as even the beft
tranflators

tranflators of them in profe fupply , avoiding all
materiall detractions from words or fence. The
word ך which wee tranflate *and* as it is redun-
dant fometime in the Hebrew, foe fomtime
(though not very ofren) it hath been left out
and yet not then , if the fence were not faire
without it.

As for our tranflations, wee have with our
englifh Bibles (to which next to the Originall
wee have had refpect) ufed the Idioms of our
owne tongue in ftead of Hebraifmes, left
they might feeme englifh barbarifmes.
Synonimaes wee ufe indifferently; as *folk* for *people*, and *Lord* for *Iehovah*, and fomtime (though
feldome) *God* for *Iehovah*; for which (as for
fome other interpretations of places cited in the
new Teftament) we have the fcriptures authority
pf. 14. with 53. Heb. 1. 6. with pfalme 97. 7.
Where a phrafe is doubtfull wee have followed
that which (in our owne apprehenfio) is moft genu
ine & edifying :

Somtime wee have contracted, fomtime
dilated the fame hebrew word , both for the
fence and the verfe fake : which dilatation
wee conceive to be no paraphrafticall addition
no more then the contraction of a true and full
tranflation to be any unfaithfull detraction or di-
minution: as when wee dilate *who healeth* and
fay *he it is who healeth*; foe when wee contract,
thofe that ftand in awe of God and fay *Gods fearers*.

Laftly. Becaufe fome hebrew words have a

** 3   more

more full and emphaticall signification then any one english word can or doth somtime expresse, hence wee have done that somtime which faithfull tranflators may doe, *viz.* not only to tranflate the word but the emphafis of it; as אל *mighty God*, for *God*. ברך *humbly bleffe* for *bleffe*; *rife to stand*, pfalm 1. for *stand truth and faithfullnes* for *truth*. Howbeit, for the verfe fake wee doe not alway thus, yet wee render the word truly though not fully; as when wee somtime fay *retoyce* for *shout for ioye*.

As for all other changes of numbers, senfes, and characters of fpeech, they are fuch as either the hebrew will unforcedly beare, or our englifh forceably calls for, or they no way change the fence; and fuch are printed ufually in an other character.

If therefore the verfes are not alwayes fo fmooth and elegant as fome may defire or expect; let them confider that Gods Altar needs not our pollifhings: Ex. 20. for wee have refpected rather a plaine tranflation, then to fmooth our verfes with the fweetnes of any paraphrafe, and foe have attended Confcience rather then Elegance, fidelity rather then poetry, in tranflating the hebrew words into englifh language, and Davids poetry into englifh meetre;

that

Preface.

that foe wee may fing in Sion the Lords
fongs of prayfe according to his owne
will, untill hee take us from hence,
and wipe away all our teares, &
bid us enter into our mafters
ioye to fing eternall
Halleluiahs.

THE PSALMES
In Metre

PSALME I

O Bleſſed man, that in th'advice
of wicked doeth not walk:
nor ſtand in ſinners way, nor ſit
in chayre of ſcornfull folk.

2 But in the law of Iehovah,
is his longing delight:
and in his law doth meditate,
by day and eke by night.

3 And he ſhall be like to a tree
planted by water-rivers:
that in his ſeaſon yeilds his fruit,
and his leafe never withers.

4 And all he doth, ſhall proſper well,
the wicked are not ſo:
but they are like vnto the chaffe,
which winde drives to and fro.

5 Therefore ſhall not ungodly men,
riſe to ſtand in the doome,
nor ſhall the ſinners with the juſt,
in their aſſemblie come.

6 For of the righteous men, the Lord
acknowledgeth the way:
but the way of vngodly men,
ſhall vtterly decay.

A PSALM

1

PSALM II

WHy rage the *Heathen* furiouſly?
    muſe vaine things people do;
2 Kings of the earth doe ſet themſelves,
    Princes conſult alſo:
with one conſent againſt the Lord.
    and his anoynted one.
3 Let us aſunder break their bands,
    their cords bee from us throwne.
4 Who ſits in heav'n ſhall laugh, the lord
    will mock them; then will he
5 Speak to them in his ire, and wrath:
    and vex them ſuddenlie.
6 But I annoynted have my King
    upon my holy hill
7 of Zion: The eſtabliſhed
    counſell declare I will.
  God ſpake to me, thou art my Son:
    this day I thee begot.
8 Aske thou of me, and I will give
    the Heathen for thy lot:
and of the earth thou ſhalt poſſeſſe
    the utmoſt coaſts abroad.
9 thou ſhalt them break as Potters ſherds
    and cruſh with yron rod.
10 And now yee Kings be wiſe, be learn'd
    yee Iudges of th'earth (*Heart.*)
11 Serve yee the lord with reverence,
    rejoyce in him with feare.
12 Kiſſe yee the Sonne, leſt he be wroth,
    and yee fall in the way.
when his wrath quickly burnes, oh bleſt

are all that on him stay.

Psalme 3

¶ A psalme of David when he fled from the face of Abfalom his Sonne.

O Lord, how many are my foes?
　how many up against me stand?

2 Many say to my foule noe helpe
　in God for him at any hand.

3 But thou Lord art my shield, my glory
　and the-uplifter of my head,.

4 with voyce to God I cal'd, who from
　his holy hill me answered.

5 I layd me downe, I slept, I wakt,
　for Iehovah did me up beare:

6 People that set against me round,
　ten thousand of them I'le not feare.

7 Arife o Lord, save me my God,
　for all mine enimies thou haft stroke
　upon the cheek-bone :& the teeth
　of the ungodly thou haft broke.

8 This, and all such salvation,
　belougeth vnto Iehovah;
　thy blessing is, aud let it be
　upon thine owne people. Selah.

Psalme 4

To the cheife Musician on *Neginoth*,
　a psalme of David.

GOD of my justice, when *I* call
　answer me: when diftreft
thou haft inlarg'd me, shew me grace,
　and heare thou my request.

A 2

2 Ye Sonnes of men, my glory turne
    to shame how long will you?
how long will ye love vanity,
    and still deceit pursue?
3 But know, the Lord doth for himselfe
    set by his gracious saint :
the Lord will heare when I to him
    doe poure out my complaint.
4 Be stirred up, but doe not sinne,
    consider seriouslie:
within your heart upon your bed;
    and wholly silent be
5 Let sacrifices of justice,
    for sacrifices be,
and confidently put your trust
    on Iehovah doe ye.
6 Many there be that say o who,
    will cause us good to see:
the light, Lord, of thy countenance
    let our us lifted be.
7 Thou hast put gladnesse in my heart,
    more then the time wherein
their corne, and also their new wine,
    have much increased bin.
8 In peace with him I will lye downe,
    and take my sleepe will I:
For thou Lord mak'st me dwell alone
    in confident safety.

Psalme. 5
To the cheife Musitian upon *Nehiloth*,
    a psalme of David.

*psalm

Heare thou my words and understand
my meditation, Iehovah .
My King, my God, attend the voyce
of my cry: for to thee I pray.
3 At morn Iehovah, thou shalt heare
my voyce: to thee I will addresse
4 at morn, I will looke up. For thou
art not a God lov'st wickednesse
neither shall evil with thee dwell.
5 Vaine glorious fooles before thine eyes
shall never stand: for thou hatest
all them that worke iniquities.
6 Thou wilt bring to distruction
the speakers of lying-falshood,
the lord will make to be abhor'd
the man deceitfull, and of blood .
7 But I will come into thine house
in multitude of thy mercy:
and will in feare of thee bow downe,
in temple of thy sanctity
8 Lead me forth in thy rightousnes,
because of mine observing spies,
O Iehovah doe thou thy wayes
make straight, and plaine, before mine eyes
9 For there no truth is in his mouth,
their inward part iniquities;
their throat an open sepulchre,
their tongue is bent to flatteries.
10 O God make thou them desolate
from their owne plots let them fall far,
cast them out in their heapes of sinnes,

A 3   for

for they againſt thee Rebells are.
11 And all that truſt in thee ſhall joy,
and ſhout for joy eternallie,
and thou ſhalt them protect: & they
that love thy name ſhall joy in thee.
12 For thou Iehovah, wilt beſtow
a bleſſing on the rightous one:
and wilt him crowne as with a ſheild,
with gracious acceptation.

Pſalme 6

To the chief Muſician on *Neginoth* upon
Sheminith, a pſalme of David.

LORD in thy wrath rebuke me nor,
nor in thy hot wrath chaſten me
2 Pitty me Lord, for I am weak.
Lord heale me, for my bones vext be.
3 Alſo my ſoule is troubled ſore:
how long Lord wilt thou me forſake.
4 Returne o Lord, my ſoule releaſe:
o ſave me for thy mercy ſake.
5 In death no mem'ry is of thee
and who ſhall prayſe thee in the grave?
6 I faint with groanes, all night my bed
ſwims, I with tears my couch waſht have.
7 mine eye with grief is dimme and old:
becauſe of all mine enimies.
8 But now depart away fom me,
all yee that work iniquities:
for Iehovah ev'n now hath heard
the voyce of theſe my weeping teares.
9 Iehovah heare my humble ſuit.

Iehovah

Iehovah doth receive my prayers.
10 Let all mine enimies be afham'd
and greatly troubled let them be,
yea let them be returned back,
and be afhamed fuddenlie.

Pfalme 7

Shiggaion of David which he fag to Iehovah
upō the words of Cufh the Benjamite.

O LORD my God in thee
I doe my truft repofe,
fave and deliver me from all
my perfecuting foes.

2 Left like a Lion hee
my foule in peeces teare
rending afunder, while there is
not one-deliverer.

3 Iehovah o my God
if this thing done have I:
if fo there be within my hands
wrongfull iniquity

4 If I required ill
the man with me at peace,
(yea I have him delivered
that was my foe caufleffe:)

5 Let foe purfue my foule,
and take, and tread to clay
my life: and honor in the duft
there let him wholly lay

6 Arife Lord in thy wrath
for th' enimies fierceneffe:
be thou lift up, & wake to me,

A 4.   judges

judgement thou'ld'ſt expreſſe.

7 So thee encompaſſe round
  ſhall peoples aſſembly;
and for the ſame doe thou returne,
  vnto the place on high.

8 The Lord ſhall judge the folke;
  Iehovah judge thou me.
according to my righteouſneſſe,
  and mine integritie.

9 Let ill mens malice ceaſe,
  but doe the juſt confirme,
for thou who art the righteous God
  doſt hearts and reins diſcerne.

10 For God my ſheild, the right
  in heart he ſaved hath.

11 The God that doth the rightous judge,
  yet daily kindleth wrath.

12 If he doe not returne,
  his ſword he'ſharp will whet:
his bow he bended hath, and he
  the ſame hath ready ſet.

13 For him he hath prepar'd
  the inſtruments of death,
for them that hotly pe ſecure,
  his arrows he ſharpneth.

14 Behold he travelleth
  of vaine iniquiry:
a toyleſome miſcheife he conceiv'd,
  but ſhall bring forth a lye.

15 A pit he digged in th.
  and delved deepe the ſame:

but

But fall'n he is into the ditch,
   that he himſelfe did frame.
16 His miſcheivous labour
   ſhall on his head turn downe,
and his injurious violence
   ſhall fall upon his crowne.
17 Iehovah I will prayſe
   for his juſt equity;
and I will ſing unto the name
   of Iehovah moſt high.

      Pſalme 8
  To the chiefe Muſician upon *Gittith*,
     a pſalme of David.

O, LORD our God in all the earth
   how's thy name wondrous great?
who haſt thy glorious maїſty
   above the heavens ſet.
2 out of the mouth of ſucking babes,
   thy ſtrength thou didſt ordeine,
that thou mightſt ſtill the enemy,
   and them that thee diſdaine.
3 when I thy fingers work, thy Heav'ns,
   the moone and ſtarres conſider:
4 which thou haſt ſet. What's wretched man,
   that thou doſt him remember?
or what's the Son of man, that thus
   him viſited thou haſt?
5 For next to Angells, thou haſt him
   a litle lower plac't
and haſt with glory crowned him,
   and comely majeſty:

b   6 and

3 And on thy works haſt given him,
    lordly authority.

7 All haſt thou put under his feet;
    all ſheep and oxen, yea

8 and beaſts of field. Foules of the ayre,
    and fiſhes of the ſea;
    and all that paſſe through paths of ſeas.

9   O Iehovah our Lord,
    how wondrouſly-magnificent
      is thy name through the world?

Pſalme 9

To the chiefe Muſician upon *Muth-Labben*
    a pſalme of David

LORD I'le the prayſe, with all my heart;
    thy wonders all proclaime.

2 I will be glad and joy in thee;
    moſt high, I'le ſing thy name.

3 In turning back my foes, they'le fall
    and periſh at thy ſight.

4 For thou maintaines my right,& cauſe:
    In throne ſits judging right.

5 Thou t' heathen checkſt, & th'wicked ſtroy'ſt,
    their names raz'd ever aye.

6 Thy ruines,foe, for aye are done;
    thou madſt their townes decaye;
  their memory with them is loſt.

7   Yet ever ſits the *Lord*:
    his throne to judgement he prepares.

8   With right he'l judge the world:
  he to the folke ſhall miniſter
    judgement in uprightneſſe.

9 The

9 The Lord is for th'opreſt a ſort:
a fort in times of ſtreſſe.

10 Who knowes thy name, will truſt in thee,
nor doſt thou, Lord forſake,

11 hem that thee ſeek. Pſalmes, to the Lord
that dwells in Sion, make:
declare among the folk his works.

12 For blood when he doth ſeeke,
he them remembers: nor forgets
the crying of the meeke.

(2)

13 Iehovah, mercy on me have,
from them that doe me hate
marke mine afflictions that ariſe,
thou lifſt me from deaths-gate.

14 That I may tell in the gates of
the Daughter of Sion,
thy prayſes all, and may rejoyce
in thy ſalvation.

15 The heathen are ſunk downe into
the pit that they had made:
their owne foot taken is ith'net
which privily they layd.

16 By judgement which he executes
Iehovah is made knowne:
the wickeo's inſnar'd in's owne hand work.
deepe meditation.

17 The wicked ſhall be turn'd to hell,
all lands that God forget.

18 Forgot the needy ſhall here be:
poores hope nere faild him yet.

B 2   9 Ariſe

II

19 Arise,o Lord, left men prevaile,
  judge t' heathen in thy fight.
20 That they may know they be but men,
  the nations Lord affright.   Selah

Pſalme 10

VV Hy ſtandſt thou Lord a far ? why hyd'ſt
  thy ſelfe in times of ſtreight?

2 In pride the wicked perſecutes
  the poore afflicted wight:
ſnare them in their contrived plots.

3 For of his hearts deſire
  the wicked boaſts, and covetous
  bleſſeth, ſtirting Gods ire.

4 The wicked one by reaſon of
  his countenances pride
will not ſeek *after* God: not God
  ſo all his thoughts abide.

5 his wayes doe alwayes bring forth griefe,
  on high thy judgements bee
above his ſight: his preſſing foes
  puffe at them all will hee.

6 Within his heart he thus hath ſayd,
  I moved ſhall not bee:
fro n aye to aye becauſe I *am*
  not in adverſitie

7 His mouth with curſing filled is,
  deceits,and fallacy:
u der his tongue perverſnes is,
  alſo iniquity.

8 In the cloſe places of the townes
  he ſits, in ſecret dens

he

12

he flays the harmleffe: 'gainft the poore
flyly his eyes downe bends.

9 He clofely lurks as lion lurks
  in der, the poore to catch
he lurks, & trapping them in 's net
  th' afflicted poore doth fnatch.

10 Downe doth he crowtch,& to the duft
  humbly he bowes *with-all*:
that fo a multitude of poore
  in his ftrong pawes may fall .

11 He faith in heart, God hath forgot:
  he hides his face away,
fo that he will not fee this thing
  unto eternall aye.

(2)

12 Iehovah rife thou up,o God
  lift thou thine hand on hy,
let not the meek afflicted one
  be out of memory.

13 Wherefore doth the ungodly mañ
  contemne th' almighty one?
he in his heart faith, thou wilt not
  make inquifition.

14 Thou feeft,for thou markft wrong,& fpight,
  with thy hand to repay:
the poore leavs it to thee,thou art
  of fatherleffe the ftay.

15 Break thou the arme of the wicked,
  and of the evil one.
fearch thou out his impiety,
  untill thou findeft none.

16 Iehov:

16 Iehovah king for ever is,
 and to eternall aye:
out of his land the heathen folke
 are perished away.
17 The meeke afflicted-mans desire
 Iehovah,thou dost heare:
thou firmly dost prepare their heart,
 thou makst attent thine eare.
18 To judge the fatherlesse & poore:
 that adde no more he may
sorrowfull man out of the land
 th terror to dismay.

Psalme 11
o the chiefe Musician a psalme
of David.

I In the Lord do trust;how then
 to my soule doe ye say,
as doth a litle bird unto
 your mountaine flye away?
2 For loe, the wicked bend their bow,
 their arrows they prepare
on string;to shoot in dark at them
 in heart that upright are.
3 If that the firme foundationes,
 utterly ruin'd bee:
as for the man that righteous is,
 what then performe can hee?
4 The Lord in's holy temple is,
 the Lords throne in heaven:
his eyes will view, and his eye lids
 will prove the Sonnes of men.

5 the

PSALME XI, XII.

5 The man that truly-righteous is
ev'n him the Lord will prove;
his soule the wicked hates, & him
that violence doth love.

6 Snares, fire, & brimstone he will raine,
ungodly men upon:
and burning tempest, of their cup
shall-be their portion.

7 For Iehovah that righteous is,
all righteousnesse doth love:
his countenane the upright one
beholding, doth approve.

Psalme 12

To the chiefe Musician upon *Sheminith*
a psalme of David.

HElpe Lord: for godly men doe cease:
faithfull faile men among.

2 Each to his freind speaks vanity;
with flattring lips, *and tongue*
and with a double heart they speake.

3 All flatt'ring lips the Lord
shall cut them of, with every tongue
that speaketh boasting word.

4 Thus have they sayd, we with our tongue,
prevailing pow're shall get:
are not our lips our owne. for Lord
who over us is set?

5 Thus saith the Lord, for sighs of them
that want, for poor opprest,
I'le now arise, from such as puffe,
will set him safe at rest.

B 4   6 pure

15

6 Pure are the words the Lord doth speak:
  as silver that is tryde
in earthen furnace, seven times
  that hath been purifyde.
7 Thou shalt them keep, o Lord, thou sha'
  preserve them ev'ry one,
For evermore in safety from
  this generation.
8 The wicked men on evry side
  doe walk presumptuously,
when as the vilest sons of men
  exalted are on hye.

Psalme 13
To the chiefe Musician: a psalme
of David.

O IEHOVAH, how long
  wilt thou forget me aye?
how long wilt thou thy countenance
  hide from me farre away?
2 How long shall I counsell,
  in my soule take, sorrow
in my heart dayly? o're me set
  how long shall be my foe?
3 Iehovah, o my God,
  behold me answer make,
Illuminate mine eyes, lest I
  the sleepe of death doe take.
4 Lest my foe say, I have.
  prevail'd 'gainst him: & me
those who doe trouble, doe rejoyce,
  when I shall moved bee.

5 But

16

5 But I aſured truſt
 have put in thy mercy;
my heart in thy ſalvation
 ſhall joy exceedingly.
6 Vnto Iehovah I
 will ſing, becauſe that hée,
for evil bountifully hath
 rewarded good to mee.

Pſalme 14
To the chiefe Muſician a pſalme
of Dauid.

THᴇ foole in's heart faith ther's no God:
 they are corrupt, have done
abominable-practiſes,
 that doth good there is none.

2 The Lord from heaven looked downe
 on Sonnes of men: to ſee,
if any that doth underſtand,
 that ſeeketh God there bee.

3 All are gone back, together they
 ev'n filthy are become:
and there is none that doeth good,
 noe not ſo much as one.

4 The workers of iniquityes,
 have they no knowledge all?
that eate my people: they eate bread,
 and on God doe not call.

5 There with a very grievous feare
 affrighted ſore they were,
for God in generation is
 of ſuch as righteous are,

‡   C   6 the

6 The counsell yee would make of him
that poore afflicted is,
to be asham'd & that becauſe·
the Lord his refuge is.

7 Who Iſraels health from Syon gives?
his folks captivitie
when God ſhall turne: Iacob ſhall joys
glad Iſrael ſhall be.

Pſalme 15
A pſalme of David.

IEHOVAH, who ſhall in thy tent
ſojourne, and who is hee
ſhall dwell within thy holy mount?

2 He that walks uprightlie,
And worketh juſtice, and ſpeaks truth

3 in's heart, And with his tongue
he doth not ſlander, neither doth
unto his neighbour wrong,
And 'gainſt his neighbour that doth not
take up reproachfull lyes.

4 Hee that an abject perſon is
contemn'd is in his eyes;
But he will highly honour them
that doe Iehovah feare:
and changeth not, though to his loſſe,
if that he once doe ſweare.

5 Nor gives his coyne to vſury,
and bribe he doth not take
againſt the harmeleſſe: he that doth
theſe things ſhall never ſhake.

PSALM

Pſalme 16
Michtam of David

O Mighty God, preſerve thou mee,
   for on thee doe I reſt.
2 Thou art my God, vnto the Lord
   my ſoule thou haſt profeſt:
My goodnes reacheth not to thee.
3 But to the Saints upon
   the earth & to the excellent,
   whome all my joye is on
4 They who give gifts to a ſtrange God,
   their ſorrowes multiplye:
their drink oblations of blood
   offer up will not I.
Neither will I into my lips
   the names of them take up.
5 Iehovah is the portion
   of my part, & my cup:
Thou art maintainer of my lot.
6 To me the lines fal'n bee
in pleaſant places: yea, faire is
   the heritage for mee.
7 I will Iehovah humbly-bleſſe,
   who hath mee counſelled:
yea in the nights my reines have mee,
   chaſtiſing nurtured.
8 Iehovah I have alwayes ſet
   as preſent before mee:
becauſe he is at my right hand
   I ſhall not moved bee.
9 Wherefore my heart rejoyced hath,

C 2

and

and glad is my glory:
moreover also my flesh shall
in hope lodge securely.

10 Because thou wilt not leave my soule
within the grave to bee,
nor wilt thou give thine holy one,
corruption for to see.

11 Thou wilt shew me the path of life,
of joyes abundant-store
before thy face, at thy right hand
are pleasures evermore.

Psalme 17
A Prayer of David.

HArken, o Lord, unto the right,
attend vnto my crye,
give eare vnto my pray'r, that goes
from lips that doe not lye.

2 From thy face let my judgement come:
thine eyes the right let see.

3 Thou provst mine heart, thou visitest
by night, and tryest mee.
yet nothing find'st, I have resolvd
my mouth shall not offend.

4 From mens works: by word of thy lips
I spoylers paths attend.

5 Stay my feet in thy paths, lest my
6 steps slip. I cal'd on thee,
for thou wilt heare, God, heare my speech.
incline thine eare to mee.

7 O thou that sav'st by thy right hand,
thy merveilous-mercyes,

shew

shew vnto them that trust in thee,
  from such as 'gainst them rise.

(2)

3 As apple of thine eye mee keepe:
  In thy wings shade mee hide.
9 From wicked who mee wast : my foes
  in heart are on each side.
10 Clos'd in their fat they are: & they
  speak with their mouth proudly.
11 They round us in our stepps: they set
  on earth their bow'd downe eye.
12 His likenes as a lion is,
  that greedy is to teare,
  in secret places lurking as
  hee a young lion were.
13 Him, in his sight, rise, disappoynt
  make him bow downe o Lord,
  doe thou my soule deliver from
  the wicked one, thy sword,
14 From mortall men thine hand, o Lord,
  from men that morrall are,
  and of this passing-world, who have
  within this life their share,
  with thy hid treasure furthermore
  whose belly thou fillest:
  their sonnes are fil'd,& to their babes
  of wealth they leave the rest.
15 In righteousnes, thy favour I
  shall very clearely see,
  and waking with thine image, I
  shall satisfied bee.

C 3   PSALM

PSALM XVIII

Pſalme 18

To the chiefe Muſieian, a *pſalme* of Dauid, the ſervant of
the Lord, who ſpake the words of this Song, in the day that
the Lord deliuered him from the hands of all his enemies,
& from the hand of Saule, and hee Sayde,

I L'e dearely love thee, Lord, my ſtrength.
  The Lord is my rock, and my towre,
  and my deliverer, my God,
  I 'le truſt in him *who is* my powre,
  My ſhield, & my ſalvationes-horne,

3 my high-fort; Who is prayſe worthy,
  I on the Lord will call, ſo ſhall
  I bee kept from mine enemye.

4 Deaths ſorrowes mee encompaſſed,
  mee fear'd the floods of ungodlie,

5 Hells pangs beſet me round about,
  the ſnares of death prevented mee.

6 I in my ſtreights, cal'd on the Lord,
  and to my God cry'd: he did heare
  from his temple my voyce, my crye,
  before him came, unto his eare.

7 Then th' earth ſhooke, & quak't, & moūtaines
  roots moov'd, & were ſtird at his ire,

8 Vp from his noſtrils went a ſmoak,
  and from his mouth devouring fire:
  By it the coales inkindled were.

9 Likewiſe the heavens he downe-bow
  and he deſcended, & there was
  under his feet a gloomy cloud.

10 And he on cherub rode, and flew;
  yea he flew on the wings of winde.

11 His ſecret place hee darknes made

his

his covert that him round confinde,
Dark waters, & thick clouds of skies.

12 From brightnes,that before him was,
his thickned clouds did passe away,
hayl-stones and coales of fire did passe.

13 Also Iehovah thundered,
within the heavens,the most high
likewise his angry-voyce did give,
hayl-stones, and coales of fire *did fly*.

14 Yea he did out his arrows send,
and bruising he them scattered,
and lightnings hee did multiply,
likewise he them discomfited.

15 The waters channels then were seene,
and the foundationes of the world
appear'd,at thy rebuke,at blast,
of the breath of thy nostrils Lord.

(2)

16 Hee from above sent hee me took:
me out of waters-great he drew.

17 Hee from mine enemies-strong, & from
them which me hated did rescue:
For they were mightyer then I.

18 They mee prevented in the day
of my cloudy calamity,
but for me was the Lord a stay.

19 And hee me to large place brought forth,
hee fav'd mee, for he did delight

20 in mee. The Lord rewarded me
according as I did aright,
According to the cleannesse of

my

my hands, he recompenced mee.

21 For the wayes of the Lord I kept:
nor from my God went wickedlie.

22 For all his iudgements mee before:
nor from me put i his decree.

23 With him i upright was, and kept
my selfe from mine iniquitie.

24 The Lord hath recompenced mee,
after my righteousnes therefore:
according to the cleannesse of
my hands that was his eyes before.

25 With mercifull, thou mercifull,
with upright thou deales uprightly.

25 With pure thou pure, thou also wilt
with froward turne thy selfe awry.

27 For thou wilt save th'afflicted folke:
but wilethe lofty looks suppresse.

28 For thou wilt light my lampe: the Lord,
my God will lighten my darknesse.

29 For by the i rann through a troupe,
and by my God leapt o're a wall.

30 Gods way is perfect: Gods word trydes
that trust in him hee's shield to all.

31 For who is God except the Lord?
or who a rock, our God except?

32 Its God that girdeth me with strength,
and hee doth make my way perfect.

33 Like to the hyndes he makes my feet:
and on my high place maks me stand.

34 Mine armes doe break a bow of brasse;
so well to warre he learnes my hand.

35 the

35 The shield of thy salvation
thou furthermore hast given mee:
and thy right-hand hath mee upheld,
thy meeknes made mee great to bee.

35 Vnder mee thou makst large my steps,
so that mine anckles did not slyde

37 My foes pursu'de I, & them caught:
nor turn'd I till they were destroyd.

38 I wounded them & they could not
rise up: under my feet they fell.

39 Because that thou hast girded mee
with fortitude to the battel:
Thou hast subdued under mee,
those that did up against me rise.

40 And my foes necks thou gavest mee,
that I might wast mine enemyes.

41 They cryde but there was none to save,
to God, yet with no answer meet.

42 I beat them then as dust i'th winde
and cast them out as dirt i'th street.

(4)

43 And thou from the contentions
hast of the people mee set free;
thou of the heathen mad'st me head:
people I knew not shall serve mee.

44 They'le at first hearing me obey:
strangers shall yield themselvs to mee.

45 The strangers shall consume away,
and from their closets frighted bee.

45 The Lord lives, and blest be my Rock,
let my healths God exalted bee.

D   47 Its

47 It's God for mee that vengeance works,
and brings downe people under mee .

48 Mee from mine enemies he doth save:
and above thofe that gainft me went,
thou lift'ft me up;and thou haft freed
mee from the man that's violent.

49 I with confeffion will therefore
unto thee render thankfgiving,
o Lord,among the heathen-folk;
and to thy name I'le prayfes fing.

50 He giveth great deliverance
to his King, and doth fhew mercy
to his annoynted, to David,
and to his feed eternally.

Pfalme 19

To the chiefe mufician a pfalme of David.

THe heavens doe declare
the majefty of God:
alfo the firmament fhews forth
his handy-work abroad.

2 Day fpeaks to day, knowledge
night hath to night declar'd.

3 There neither fpeach nor language is,
where their voyce is not heard.

4 Through all the earth their line
is gone forth, & unto
the utmoft end of all the world,
their fpeaches reach alfo:
A Tabernacle hee
in them pitcht for the Sun.

5 Who Bridegroom like from's chamber goes
glad

glad Giants-race 'to run.

6 From heavens utmost end,
    his courſe and compaſſing,
to ends of it, & from the heat
    thereof is hid nothing.

(2)

7 The Lords law perfect is,
    the ſoule converting back:
Gods teſtimony faithfull is,
    makes wiſe who-wiſdome-lack.

8 The ſtatutes of the Lord,
    are right, & glad the heart:
the Lords commandement is pure,
    light doth to eyes impart.

9 Iehovahs feare is cleane,
    and doth indure for ever:
the judgements of the Lord are true,
    and righteous altogether.

10 Then gold, then much fine gold,
    more to be prized are,
then hony, & the hony-comb,
    ſweeter they are by farre.

11 Alſo thy ſervant is
    admoniſhed from hence:
and in the keeping of the ſame
    is a full recompence.

12 Who can his errors know?
    from ſecret faults cleanſe mee.

13 And from preſumptuous-ſins, let thou
    kept back thy ſervant bee:
Let them not beare the rule

D 2

in me, & then shall I
be perfect, and shall cleansed bee
from much iniquity.

14 Let the words of my mouth,
and the thoughts of my heart,
be pleasing with thee, Lord, my Rock
who my redeemer art.

Psalme 20

To the chiefe Musician, a psalme of David.

IEHOVAH heare thee in the day
of sore calamity,
the name of the God of Iacob
defend thee mightily.

2 Send thee help from his holy place;
from Sion strengthen thee.

3 Minde all thy gifts, thy sacrifice
accepted let it bee.   Selah.

4 Grant thee according to thy heart,
all thy counsell fulfill.

5 In thy perfect salvation
with singing joy we will:
And we in the name of our God
our banners will erect:
when as all thy petitions
Iehovah shall effect.

6 Now I know, that Iehovah doth
save his annoynted-Deare:
with saving strength of his right hand
from his pure heav'n will heare.

7 In charrets some their confidence,
and some in horses set:

but

but we the name of Iehovah
our God will not forget.
8 They are brought downe & fal'n: but we,
rise and stand stedfastly.
9 Save Lord,& let the King us heare
when as to him we cry.
Psalme 21
To the chiefe Musician a psalme
of David.

IEHOVAH, in thy strength
the King shall joyfull bee;
and joy in thy salvation
how vehemently shall hee?
2 Thou of his heart to him
hast granted the desire:
and thou hast not witholden back,
 - what his lips did require.   Selah.
3 For thou dost with blessings
of goodnes prevent him:
thou on his head of finest gold
hast set a Diadem.
4 Of thee hee asked life,
to him thou gav'st it free,
even length of days for evermore
unto eternitie.
5 In thy salvation
his glory hath bene great:
honour, and comely dignity
thou hast upon him set.
6 For thou him blessings setst
to perpetuitie:

D 3   thou

Thou makſt him with thy countenance
   exceeding glad to bee.
7 Becauſe that in the Lord
   the King doth truſt, & hee
through mercy of the higheſt one,
   ſhall not removed bee.
8 The Lord ſhall finde out all
   that are thine enemies:
thy right hand alſo ſhall finde out
   thoſe that doe thee deſpiſe.
9 Thou ſetſt as fiery oven
   them in times of thine ire:
the Lord will ſwallow them in's wrath
   and them conſume with fire.
10 Thou wilt deſtroy the fruit,
   that doth proceed of them,
out of the earth: & their ſeed from
   among the Sonnes of men.
11 Becauſe they evill have
   intended againſt thee:
a wicked plot they have deviſ'd,
   but ſhall not able bee.
12 For thou wilt as a butt
   them ſet; & thou wilt place
thine arrows ready on thy ſtring.
   full right againſt their face.
13 Lord, in thy fortitude
   exalted bee on high:
and wee will ſing; yea prayſe with pſalmes
   thy mighty powr will wee.

PSAL.

Pſalme 22
To the chiefe muſician upon *Aijeleth Shahar*
a pſalme of David.

M Y God, my God, wherefore haſt thou
forſaken mee? & why,
art thou ſo farre from helping mee,
from the words of my cry?

2 O my God, I doe cry by day,
but mee thou doſt not heare;
and eke by night, & unto mee
no quiet reſt is there.

3 Nevertheleſſe thou holy art,
who conſtantly doſt dwell,
within the thankfull prayſes of
thy people Iſraell.

4 Our fore-fathers in thee have put
aſſured confidence:
they truſted have, & thou to them
didſt give deliverance.

5 Vnto thee they did cry aloud,
and were delivered:
in thee they put their confidence,
and were not confounded.

6 But I a worme, & not a man,
of men an opprobrie,
and alſo of the people am
deſpiſ'd contemptuouſlie.

7 All they that doe upon mee look,
a ſcoffe at mee doe make:
they with the lip doe make a mow,
the head in ſcorne they ſhake,

upo

8 Vpon the Lord he rold himſelfe,
    let him now rid him quite:
let him deliver him, becauſe
    in him he doth delight.

9 But thou art hee that me out of
    the belly forth didſt take:
when I was on my mothers breaſts,
    to hope thou didſt mee make.

10 Vnto thee from the tender-womb
    committed been have I:
yea thou haſt been my mighty-God
    from my mothers belly.

(2)

11 Be thou not farre away from mee,
    for tribulation
exceeding great is neere at hand,
    for helper there is none.

12 Mee many buls on every ſide
    about have compaſſed:
the mighty-buls of Baſhan have
    mee round invironed.

13 They have with their wide-opened-mouths
    ſo gaped mee upon;
like as it were a ravening
    and a roaring Lion.

14 As water I am poured-out,
    and all my bones ſundred:
my heart in midſt of my bowels,
    is like to wax melted.

15 My ſtrength like a potſherd is dryde;
    and my tongue faſt cleaveth

                unto

unto my jawes,& thou haſt brought
me to the duſt of death.

16 For dogs have compaſt me abour;
th' aſſembly me beſet
of the wicked; they pierced through
my hands, alſo my feet.

17 My bones I may them number all;
they lookt,they did me view.

18 My cloths among them they did parn
and lot for my coat threw.

19 But thou Lord be not far, my ſtrength,
to help me haſten thou.

20 My ſoule from ſword,my darling from
the powre of dogs reſcue.

21 And from the mouth of the Lion
give me ſalvation free:
for thou from hornes ofVnicornes
anſver haſt given mee.

22 Thy name,I will declare to them
that Brethren are to mee:
in midſt of congregation
I will give prayſe to thee.

(3)
23 Yee that doe feare the Lord prayſe him,
all Iacobs ſeed prayſe yee,
him glorify,& dread him all
yee Iſraels ſeed that bee.

24 For he the poors affliction
loaths not,nor doth deſpiſe;
nor hides his face from him, but hears
when unto him hee cryes.

E   25 concern-

25 Concerning thee shall be my prayse
  in the great assembly:
 before them that him reverence
  performe my vowes will I.
26 The meek shall eat & be suffic'd:
  Iehovah prayse shall they
 that doe him seek: your heart shall live
  unto perpetuall aye.
27 All ends of th'earth remember shall
  and turne unto the Lord:
 and thee all-heathen-families
  to worship shall accord.
28 Because unto Iehovah doth
  the kingdome appertaine:
 and he among the nations
  is ruler Soveraigne.
29 Earths-fat-ones, eat & worship shall:
  all who to dust descend,
 (though none can make alive his soule)
  before his face shall bend.
30 With service a posterity
  him shall attend upon:
 to God it shall accounted bee
  a generation.
31 Come shall they, & his righteousnes
  by them declar'd shall bee,
 unto a people yet unborne,
  that done this thing hath hee.

   23   A Psalme of David.

THe Lord to mee a shepheard is,
  want therefore shall not I.

                              2 Hee

2 Hee in the folds of tender-graffe,
    doth caufe mee downe to lie:
  To waters calme me gently leads
3   Reftore my foule doth hee:
  he doth in paths of righteoufnes:
    for his names fake leade mee.
4 Yea though in valley of deaths fhade
    I walk, none ill I'le feare:
  becaufe thou art with mee, thy rod,
    and ftaffe my comfort are.
5 For mee a table thou haft fpread,
    in prefence of my foes:
  thou doft annoynt my head with oyle,
    my cup it over-flowes.
6 Goodnes & mercy furely fhall
    all my dayes follow mee:
  and in the Lords houfe I fhall dwell
    fo long as dayes fhall bee.

Pfalme 24
A pfalme of david.

THe earth Iehovahs is,
    and the fulneffe of it:
  the habitable world, & they
    that there upon doe fit.
2 Becaufe upon the feas,
    hee hath it firmly layd:
  and it upon the water-floods
    moft follidly hath ftayd.
3 The mountaine of the Lord,
    who fhall thereto afcend?
  and in his place of holynes,

E 5   who

who is it that shall stand?
4 The cleane in hands, & pure
   in heart;to vanity
who hath not lifted up his soule,
   nor sworne deceitfully.
5 From God he shall receive
   a benediction,
and righteousnes from the strong-God
   of his salvation.
6 This is the progenie
   of them that seek thy face:
of them that doe inquire for him:
   of Iacob 'tis the race.   Selah.
7 Yee gates lift-up your heads,
   and doors everlasting,
be yee lift up: & there into
   shall come the glorious-King
8 Who is this glorious King?
   Iehovah, puissant,
and valiant, Iehovah is
   in battel valiant.
9 Yee gates lift-up your heads,
   and doors everlasting,
doe yee lift-up: & there into
   shall come the glorious-King.
10 Who is this glorious-King?
   loe, it is Iehovah
of warlike armies, hee the King
   of glory is; Selah.
          Psalme 25
      A psalme of David.

                    PSALM

PSALME XXV.

I Lift my foule to thee o Lord.
  My God I truft in thee,
let mee not be afham'd: nor let
  my foes joy over mee.

3 Yea, all that wait on thee fhall not,
   be fill'd with fhamefulnes:
but they fhall be afhamed all,
  who without caufe tranfgreffe.

4 Thy wayes, Iehovah, make mee know,
  thy paths make me difcerne.

5 Caufe mee my fteps to order well,
  in thy truth, & mee learne,
For thou God of my faving health,
  on thee I wait all day.

6 Thy bowels, Lord, & thy mercyes
  minde; for they are for aye.

7 Sinnes of my youth remember not,
  neither my trefpaffes:
after thy mercy minde thou mee
  o Lord for thy goodnes.

8 Good and upright God is, therefore
  will finners teach the way.

9 The meek he'le guide in judgement: &
  will teach the meek his way.

10 Iehovahs paths they mercy are,
   all of them truth alfo;
to them that keep his covenant,
  and teftimonies do.

(2)

11 For thy names fake o Iehovah,
   freely doe thou remitt

E 3

mine owne perverfe iniquitie:
  becaufe that great is it.
12 Who fears the Lord, him hee will teach
  the way that he fhall chufe.
13 his foule fhall dwell at eafe, his feed
  as heirs the earth fhall vfe.
14 The fecret of God is with thofe
  that doe him reverence:
and of his covenant he them
  will give intelligence.
15 Mine eyes continually are
  upon Iehovah fet:
for it is hee that will bring forth
  my feet out of the net.
16 Vnto me-wards turne thou thy face,
  and on mee mercy fhow:
becaufe I folitary am
  afflicted poore alfo.
17 My hearts troubles inlarged are;
  from my diftreffe me bring.
18 See mine affliction,& my paine;
  and pardon all my fin.
19 Mark my foes; for they many are,
  and cruelly mee hate,
20 My foule keep,free mee;nor let mee
  be fham'd,who on thee wait.
21 Let foundnes,& uprightneffe keep
  mee: for I truft in thee.
22 Ifrael from his troubles all,
  o God, doe thou fet free,
26 A *pfalme* of david.

PSAl.

IVdge mee, o Lord, for I have walkt
in mine integrity:
and I have trufted in the Lord,
therefore flyde fhall not I.

2 Examine mee, Lord, & mee prove;
my reins, & my heart try.

3 For thy grace is before mine eyes;
and in thy truth walk I.

4 I fat not with vaine men, nor goe
with men themfelves that hide.

5 Evill mens company I hate:
nor will with vile abide.

6 In cleanneffe, Lord, I'le wafh mine hands,
fo I'le thine altar round:

7 That I may preach with thankfull-voyce,
and all thy prayfes found.

8 The habitation of thy houfe,
Lord, dearly love doe I,
the place and tabernacle of
thy glorious majefty.

9 My foule with finners gather not,
with men of blood my life.

10 In whofe hand 's guile, in whofe right hand
bribery is full rife.

11 Redeeme, & pitty mee; for I'le
walk in mine uprightneffe.

12 My foot ftands right: in th'affembly
I will Iehovah bleffe.

27 *A* Pfalme of David.

THe Lord my light, & my health is,
what fhall make me difmaid?

ths

PSALM XXVII.

The Lord is my lifes-ftrength, of whom
   fhould I *then* be afrayd?
2 When wicked men, mine enemies,
   and my foes in battel,
against mee come, to eate my flefh,
   themfelves ftumbled & fell.
3 If that an hoaft against mee camp,
   my heart undaunted is:
if war against mee fhould arife,
   I am fecure in this.
4 One thing of God I afked have,
   which I will ftill requeft:
that I may in the houfe of God,
   all dayes of my life reft:
To fee the beauty of the Lord,
   and in his Temple feeke.
5 For in his tent in th'evill-day,
   hidden hee will mee keepe:
Hee will me hide in fecrecy
   of his pavillion:
and will me highly lift upon
   the rocks-munition.
6 Moreover at this-time my head
   lifted on high fhall bee,
above mine enemies, who doe
   about encompaffe mee.
Therefore in's tent I'le facrifice,
   of joyè an offering,
unto Iehovah, fing will I,
   yea, I will prayfes fing.

When

(2)

7 When as I with my voyce doe cry,
   mee,o Iehovah,heare,
have mercy alſo upon mee,
   and unto mee anſwer.
8 *When thou didſt ſay,* ſeek yee my face,
   my heart ſaydˀunto thee,
thy countenance,o Iehovah,
   it ſhall be ſought by mee.
9 Hide not thy face from mee, nor off
   in wrath thy ſervant caſt:
God of my health, leave, leave not mee.
   my helper been thou haſt.
10 My father & my mother both
   though they doe mee forſake,
yet will Iehovah gathering
   unto himſelfe me take.
11 Iehovah, teach thou mee the way,
   and be a guide to mee
in righteous path, becauſe of them
   that mine obſervers bee.
12 Give mee not up unto the will
   of my ſtreight-enemies:
for witneſſe falſe againſt me ſtand
   and breath out cruelties.
13 *I ſhould baue ſainted,* had not I
   believed for to ſee,
Iehovahs goodnes in the land
   of them that living bee.
14 Doe thou upon Iehovah waite:
   bee ſtabliſhed, & let

F.

hine

thine heart be ftrengthened,& thine hope
upon Iehovah fet.

Pfalme 2ᵉ.

A pfalme of David.

IEHOVAH,unto thee I cry.
my Rock,be thou not deafe me froᵐ
left thou be dumb from mee & I
be like them downe to pit that go.

2 Heare thou the voyce of my requeft
for grace, when unto thee I cry:
when I lift up mine hands unto
thine Oracle of Sanctity.

3 With ill men draw me not away,
with workers of unrighteoufnes,
that with their neighbours peace doe fpeak.
but in their hands is wickednes.

4 Give thou to them like to their works
and like the evill of their deeds:
give them like to their handy-works,
and render unto them their meeds.

5 Becaufe unto Iehovahs work
they did not wife-attention yeild.
neither unto his handy work,
them he will waft,but not up-build.

6 The Lord be bleft,for he hath heard
the voyce of my requefts for grace.

7 God is my ftrength,my fhield,in him
my heart did truft, & helpt I was:
Therefore my heart will gladnes fhew
and with my fong I le him confeffe.

8 The Lord of his annoynted ones

their

42

their strength, & towre of safety is.
9 Salvation to thy people give,
and blesse thou thine inheritance,
and ev'n unto eternity
doe thou them feed & them advance.

This. After the common tunes.

Save *Lord*, thy people, & doe thou
blesse thine inheritance:
and unto all eternity
them feed & them advance.

Psalme 29
A psalme of David.

VNto the Lord doe yee ascribe
(o Sonnes of the mighty)
unto the Lord doe yee ascribe
glory & potency.
2 Vnto the Lord doe yee ascribe
his names glorious renowne,
in beauty of his holynes
unto the Lord bow downe.
3 The mighty voyce of Iehovah
upon the waters is:
the God of glory thundereth,
God on great waters is.
4 Iehovahs voyce is powerfull,
Gods voyce is glorious,
5 Gods voyce breaks Cedars:yea God breaks
Cedars of Lebanus.
6 He makes them like a calfe to skip:

F 2

the

43

the mountaine Lebanon,
and like to a young Vnicorne
the hill of Syrion.

7 Gods voyce divides the flames of fire.

8 Iehovahs voyce doth make
the defart fhake: the Lord doth caufe
the Cadefh-defart fhake.

9 The Lords voyce makes the hindes to calve,
and makes the forreft bare:
and in his temple every one
his glory doth declare.

10 The Lord fate on the flouds: the Lord
for ever fits as King.

11 God to his folk gives ftrength: the Lord
his folk with peace bleffing.

Pfalme 30

A Pfalme & Song, at the dedication
of the houfe of David.

IEHOVAH, I will thee extoll,
for thou haft lift up mee;
and over mee thou haft not made
my foes joyfull to bee.

2 O Lord my God, to thee I cry'de
and thou haft made mee whole.

3 Out of the grave, o Iehovah,
thou haft brought up my foule:
Thou mad'ft mee live, I went not downe

4 to pit. Sing to the Lord,
(yee his Saints)& give thanks when yee
his holynes record.

5 For but a moment in his wrath,

'life

life in his love doth ftay:
weeping may lodge with us a night
but joye at break of day.

6 I fayd in my profperity,
I fhall be moved never.

7 Lord by thy favour thou haft made
my mountaine ftand faft ever:
Thou hidft thy face, I troubled was.

8 I unto thee did cry,
o Lord: alfo my humble fuit
unto the Lord made I.

9 What gaine is in my blood; when I
into the pit goe downe?
fhall duft give glory unto thee?
fhall it thy truth make knowne?

10 Doe thou mee o Iehovah, heare,
and on mee mercy have:
Iehovah, o bee thou to mee
an helper me to fave.

11 Thou into dancing for my fake
converted haft my fadnes:
my fackcloth thou unloofed haft,
and girded me with gladnes:

12 That fing to thee my glory may,
and may not filent bee:
o Lord my God, I will give thanks
for evermore to thee.

Pfalme 31
To the chief Mufician, a pfalme
of David.

F 3   PSALM

IN thee, o Lord, I put my truſt,
   let me be ſhamed never:
according to thy righteouſnes
   o doe thou mee deliver.

2 Bow downe to mee thine eare,with ſpeed
   let mee deliverance have:
be thou my ſtrong rock, for an houſe
   of defence mee to ſave.

3 Becauſe thou unto mee a rock
   and my fortreſſe wilt bee:
therefore for thy names ſake doe-thou,
   leade mee & guide thou mee.

4 Doe thou mee pull out of the net.
   which they have for mee layd
ſo privily:becauſe that thou
   art to mee a ſure ayd.

5 Into thy hands my ſpirit I
   repoſing doe commit:
Iehovah God of verity,
   thou haſt redeemed it.

6 I hated them that have regard
   to lying vanity:

7 but I in God truſt. I'le be glad,
   and joy in thy mercy:
Becauſe thou haſt conſidered
   my afflicting diſtreſſe;
thou haſt my ſoule acknowledged
   in painfull anguiſhes;

8 And thou haſt not incloſed mee
   within the enemies hand:
thou mad'ſt my feet within the place

of

PSALME xxxi.

of liberty to ſtand.

(2)

9 Have mercy upon mee,o Lord,
  for in diſtreſſe am *I*,
  with grief mine eye conſumed is,
  my ſoule & my belly.
10 For my life with grief & my years
  with ſighs are conſumed:
  becauſe of my ſin,my ſtrength failes,
  and my bones are waſted.
11 To all my foes I was a ſcorne,
  chiefly my neighbours to;
  a feare to freinds: they that ſaw mee
  without, did flye me fro.
12 I am forgot as a dead man
  that's out of memory:
  and like a veſſel that is broke
  ev'n ſuch a one am I.
13 Becauſe that I of many men
  the ſlandering did heare,
  round about me on every ſide
  there was exceeding feare:
  While as that they did againſt mee
  counſell together take,
  they craftily have purpoſed
  my life away to make.
14 But o Iehovah,I in thee
  my confidence have put
15 I ſayd thou art my God. My times
  within thy hand *are ſhut*:
  From the hands of mine enemies

doe

doe thou deliver mee,
and from the men who mecagainst
    my persecuters bee.
            (5)
16 Thy countenance for to shine forth
    upon thy servant make:
  o give to me salvation
    even for thy mercy sake.
17 Let me not be asham'd, o Lord,
    for cal'd on thee I have:
  let wicked men be sham'd, let them
    be silent in the grave.
18 Let lying lips be silenced,
    that against men upright
  doe speak such things as greivous are,
    in pride, & in despight.
19 How great 's thy goodnes, thou for the
    that feare thee hast hidden:
  which thou work'st for them that thee trust,
    before the Sonnes of men.
20 Thou in the secret of thy face,
    shalt hide them from mans pride:
  in a pavillion, from the strife
    of tongues, thou wilt them hide.
21 O let Iehovah blessed be;
    for he hath shewed mee
  his loving kindnes wonderfull
    in a fenced-cittie.
22 For I in hast say, I, I am cast..
    from the sight of thine eyes:
  yet thou heardst the voyce of my suit,

                                    when

when to thee were my cryes.

23 O love the Lord all ye his Saints
    becaufe the Lord doth guard
the faithfull, but the proud doer
    doth plenteoufly reward.

24 See that yee be encouraged,
    and let your heart wax ftrong:
all wholoever hopefully
    doe for Iehovah long.

    32 A *pfalme* of David, Mafchil.

O Bleffed is the man who hath
    his trefpaffe pardoned,
and he *whofe* aberration
    is wholly covered,

2 O bleffed is the man to whom
    the Lord imputes not fin:
and he who fuch a fpirit hath
    that guile is not therein.

3 When I kept filence then my bones,
    began to weare away,
with age, by meanes of my roaring
    continuing all the day

4 For day & night thy hand on mee,
    heavily did indure:
into the drought of Summer time
    turned is my moifture.   Selah,

5 Mine aberration unto thee
    I have acknowledged,
and mine iniquity I have
    not clofely covered:
Againft my felfe my fin, fayd I,
        G   I will

I will to God confesse,
and thou didst the iniquitie
forgive of my trespasse.   Selah.
6 For this each godly one to thee
in finding time shall pray.
surely in floods of waters great,
come nigh him shall not they.
7 Thou art my hyding-place, thou shalt
from trouble save me out:
thou with songs of deliverance
shalt compasse me about.
8 I will instruct thee, also teach
thee in the way will I
which thou shalt goe: I will to thee
give counsell with mine eye.
9 Like to the horse & mule, which have
noe knowledge be not yee:
whose mouths are held with bridle-bit,
that come not neere to thee.
10 To those men that ungodly are,
their sorrows doe abound:
but him that trusteth in the Lord,
mercy shall compasse round.
11 Be in Iehovah joyfull yee,
yee righteous ones rejoyce,
and all that are upright in heart
shout yee with joyfull voyce.
               psalme 33
Ee just in God rejoyce,
    prayse well th'upright doth sute:
Prayse God with Harp, with psaltry sing

to him, on ten ftring'd lute.
3 Sing to him a new fong,
 aloud play fkilfully.
4 For the Lords word is right: and all
 his works in varity.
5 He loveth righteoufnes,
 and alfo equity:
 the earth replenifhed is with
 the Lords benignity.
6 By the word of the Lord
 the heavens had their frame,
and by the fpirit of his mouth,
 all the hoft of the fame,
7 The waters of the feas,
 he gathers as an heape;
together as in ftore-houfes
 he layeth up the deepe.
8 Be all the earth in feare,
 becaufe of Iehovah:
let all the dwellers of the world
 before him ftand in awe.
9 Becaufe he did but fpeak
 the word, & it was made.
he gave out the commandement,
 and it was firmly ftay'd.
10 The Lord to nought doth bring
 the nations counfell; hee
devifes of the people makes
 of none effect to bee.
11 The counfell of the Lord
 abide for ever fhall,

G 4   the

the cogitations of his heart
to generations all.

(2)

12 O blessed nation,
vhose God Iehovah is:
and people whom for heritage
chosen hee hath for his.

13 The Lord from heaven looks,
all Sonnes of men views well.

14 From his firme dwelling hee looks forth,
on all that on earth dwell.

15 The hearts of all of them
alike he fashioneth:
and all their operations
he well considereth.

16 By multitude of hoaſt
there is no King saved:
nor is by multitude of ſtrength
the ſtrong delivered.

17 A horſe a vaine thing is
to be a saviour:
nor ſhall he work deliverance
by greatnes of his power.

18 On them that doe him feare
loe, is Iehovahs eye:
upon them that doe place their hope
on his benignity.

19 To save alive in dearth,
and their soule from death free.

20 Our soule doth for Iehovah wayt,
our help, & ſhield is hee:

21 ſor

21 For our heart joyes in him:
   for in's pure name truſt wee.
22 Let thy mercy (Lord)be on us:
   like as we truſt in thee.

Pſalme 34

A *pſalme* of David,whē he changed his behaviour
   before Abimelech,who drove him away
   & he departed.

I Le bleſſe God alwayes,his prayſe ſhall
   ſtill in my mouth be had.
2 My ſoule ſhall boaſt in God:the meeke
   ſhall heare *this* & bee glad.
3 Exalt the Lord with mee,his name
   let us together advance.
4 I ſought,God heard, who gave from all
   my fears deliverance.
5 Him they beheld, & light'ned were,
   nor ſham'd were their faces.
6 This poore man cry'd,the Lord him heard,
   and freed from all diſtreſſe.
7 His camp about them round doth pitch
   the Angell of the Lord;
   who doe him feare;and to them doth
   deliverance afford.
8 O taſt,alſo conſider yee,
   that God is good:o bleſt,
   that man is ever whoſe hope doth
   for ſafety in him reſt.
9 O ſtand in feare of Iehovah,
   his holy ones who bee.
   becauſe that ſuch as doe him feare

G 3

noe

not any want shall see.
20 The Lions young doe suffer lack,
    and suffer-hungering:
  but they that seek Iehovah, shall
    not want any good thing
                (2)
11 I will you teach to feare the Lord:
    come children hark to mee.
12 Who is the man that willeth life:
    and loves good dayes to see?
13 Thy tongue from evill,& thy lips
    from speaking guile keep thou.
14 Depart from evill & doe good:
    seek peace,and it follow.
15 Vpon the men that righteous are
    the Lord doth set his eye:
  and likewise he doth bow his eare
    when unto him they cry.
16 Iehovahs face is set against
    them that doe wickedly:
  that he of them from off the earth
    may cut the memory.
17 They cry'd, God heard,& set them free,
    from their distresses all.
18 To broken hearts the Lord is neere,
    and contrite save he shall.
19 The just mans sorrows' many are,
    from all God sets him free.
20 Hee kepeth all his bones, that none
    of them shall broken bee.
21 Evill shall certainly bring death,
    the wicked man upon: and

and those that hate the just shall come
to desolation.

22 The soules of them that doe him serve,
   Iehovah doth redeeme:
nor any shall be desolate,
   that put their trust in him.

     35 *A psalme* of David.

PLead, Lord, with them that with me plead:
   fight against them that fight with mee.
2 Of shield & buckler take thou hold,
   stand up my helper for to bee.
3   Draw out the speare & stop the way
   'gainst them that my pursuers bee:
   and doe thou say unto my soule
   I am salvation unto thee.
4   Let them confounded be,& sham'd,
   that seek my soule how they may spill:
   let them be turned back & sham'd
   that in their thoughts devise mine ill.
5   As chaffe before the winde, let them
   be,& Gods Angell them driving.
6 Let their way dark & slippery bee,
   and the Lords Angell them chasing.
7   For in a pit without a cause,
   they hidden have for me a net:
   which they without a cause have digg'd
   that they there in my soule may get.
8   Let unknowne ruin come on him,
   and let his net that he doth hide,
   himselfe insnare: let him into
   the very same destruction slyde,

                My

9   My foule fhall in the Lord be glad:
in his falvation joyfull bee

10 And all my bones fhall alfo fay,
o Lo d who is like unto thee?
  Who from the ftronger then himfelfe
the poore afflicted fetteft free:
the poore afflicted & needy,
from fuch as fpoylers of him bee.
(2)

11 Falfe witneffes did up arife:
what I knew not they charg'd on mee.

12 Evill for good they mee repay'd,
whereby my foule might fpoyled bee,

13 But I, when they were fick, was cloath'd
with fackcloath,& I afflicted
my foule with fafting,& my pray'r
into my bofom returned.

14 I walked as if he had been
my neere freind or mine owne brother:
I heavily bow'd downe as one
that mourneth for his owne mother.

15 But they in mine adverfity
rejoyced, & they gathered
themfelves together: yea abjects
themfelves againft mee gathered;
  And I was ignorant *hereof*;
and they unceafantly mee teare,

16 With hypocrites, mockers in feafts;
at me their teeth they gnafhing were.

17 How long o Lord wilt thou look on?
my foule from their deftructions,

doe

o doe thou set at liberty,
mine only one from the Lions.

18 I freely will give thanks to thee
within the congregation great:
and I thy prayses will set forth
where there be many people met.

19 Those that are wrongfully my foes,
let them not rejoyce over mee:
neither let them wink with the eye,
that are my haters causlesly.

20 Because that they doe not speak peace:
but in their thoughts they doe invent
deceitfull matters against them
that in the land for peace are bent.

21 Gainst me they op'ned their mouths wide,
& sayd,ah,ah our eye it saw.

22 Thou saw'st it (Lord) hold not thy peace:
Lord,from me be not far away.

23 Stirre up & wake to my judgement,
my God & my Lord, to my plea.

24 After thy justice,judge me,Lord
my God,lest or'e me joy should they.

25 Let them not say within their hearts,
aha,our soules desire have wee:
we now have swallowed him up.
o let them never say of mee.

25 Sham'd let them be & confounded
joyntly,who at my hurt are glad:
let them that 'gainst me magnify,
with shame & dishonour be clad.

27 Let them for joy shout,& be glad

H   that

that favour doe my righteous cause:
yea, let them say continually,
extolled be the Lord with prayse,
   Who doth in the prosperity
of his servants his pleasure stay
29 And my tongue of thy justice shall,
and of thy prayse speake all the day.

Psalme 36.

To the chief Musician a psalme of David,
the servant of the Lord.

THe trespasse of the wicked one
   saith in assured-wise:
within my heart, the feare of God
   is not before his eyes.
2 For in his eyes he sooths himselfe:
   his sin is found meane while
3 hatefull. The words of his mouth are
   iniquity & guile:
He to be wise,to doe good leaves.
4   He mischief plotts on's bed,
he sets himselfe in way not good:
   he hath not ill hated.

(2)

5 Thy mercy (Lord)in heaven is,
   to clouds thy faithfullnes.
6 Thy judgements a great deep, like great
   mountains thy righteousnes:
Thou savest man & beast,o Lord.
7   How pretious is thy grace,
therefore in shadow of thy wings
   mens sonnes their trust doe place.

They

8 They of the fatnes of thy houſe
   unto the full ſhall take:
and of the river of thy joyes
   to drink thou ſhalt them make.
9 For with thee is the ſpring of life:
   in thy light wee'll ſee light.
10 To them that know thee ſtretch thy grace;
   to right in heart thy right.
11 Let no proud foot againſt me come,
   nor wicked hand move mee.
12 Wrong doers there are fal'n: caſt downe,
   and rayſ'd they cannot bee,

     37 A Pſalme of David.

FRet not thy ſelfe becauſe of thoſe
  that evill workers bee,
nor envious bee againſt the men
   that work iniquitie.
2 For like unto the graſſe they ſhall
   be cut downe, ſuddenly:
and like unto the tender herb
   they withering ſhall dye.
3 Vpon the Lord put thou thy truſt,
   and bee thou doing good,
ſo ſhalt thou dwell within the land,
   and ſure thou ſhalt have food.
4 See that thou ſet thy hearts delight
   alſo upon the Lord,
and the deſyers of thy heart
   to thee he will afford:
5 Truſt in the Lord: & hee'l it work,
   to him commit thy way.

     H 2

          6 As

6 As.light thy justice hee'l bring forth,
    thy judgement as noone day.
7 Rest in Iehovah, & for him
    with patience doe thou stay:
  fret not thy selfe becaufe of him
    who profpers in his way,
  Nor at the man, who brings to paffe
    the crafts he doth devife.
8 Ceafe ire, & wrath leave: to doe ill
    thy felfe fret in no wife.
9 For evil docrs fhall be made
    by cutting downe to fall:
  but thofe that wayt upon the Lord,
    the land inherit fhall.

(2)

10 For yet a litle while, & then
    the wicked fhall not *bee*:
  yea, thou fhalt diligently mark
    his place, & it not fee.
11 But meek ones the inheritance
    fhall of the earth poffeffe:
  alfo they fhall themfelves delight
    in multitude of peace.
12 The wicked plotts againft the juft,
    gnafhing at him his teeth.
13 The Lord fhall laugh at him: becaufe
    his day coming he feeth.
14 The wicked have drawne out their fword,
    & bent their bowe have they,
  to caft the poor & needy downe,
    to kill th'upright in way.

15 their

15 Their sword shall enter their owne heart,
   their bowes shall broken bee.
16 **The just mans little, better** *is*
   then wickeds treasurie.
17 For th'armes of wicked shall be broke:
   the Lord the just doth stay.
18 The Lord doth know upright mens dayes:
   and their lot is for aye.
19 Neither shall they ashamed bee
   in any time of ill:
 and when the dayes of famine come,
   they then shall have their fill.
20 But wicked,& foes of the Lord
   as lambs fat shall decay:
 they shall consume:yea into smoake
   they shall consume away.

(3)

21 The man ungodly borroweth,
   but he doth not repay:
 but he that righteous is doth shew
   mercy,& gives away.
22 For such as of him blessed bee,
   the earth inherit shall,
 and they that of him cursed are,
   by cutting downe shall fall.
23 The foot-steps of a godly man
   they are by Iehovah
 established: & also hee
   delighteth in his way.
24 Although he fall,yet shall he not
   be utterly downe cast:

H 3   because

because Iehovah with his hand
  doth underprop him faſt.
25 I have been young & now am old;
  yet have I never ſeen
the juſt man left, nor that his ſeed
  for bread have beggars been.
26 But every day hee's mercifull,
  and lends: his ſeed is bleſt.
27 Depart from evill,& doe good:
  and ever dwell at reſt.
28 Becauſe the Lord doth judgement love,
  his Saints forſakes not hee;
kept ever are they: but cut off
  the ſinners ſeed ſhall bee.
29 The juſt inherit ſhall the land,
  and therein ever dwell.
30 The juſt mans mouth wiſdome doth ſpeak,
  his tongue doth judgement tell.
31 The law of his God is in's heart:
  none of his ſteps ſlideth.
32 The wicked watcheth for the juſt,
  and him to ſlay ſeeketh .
33 Iehovah will not ſuch a one
  relinquiſh in his hand,
neither will he condemne him when
  adjudged he doth ſtand.
    (4)
34 Wayt on the Lord,& keep his way,
  and hee ſhall thee exalt
th'earth to inheri': when cut off
  the wicked ſee thou ſhalt.

            35 The

35 The wicked men I have beheld
    in mighty pow'r to bee:
  alfo himfefe fpreading abroad
    like to a green-bay-tree.
36 Neverthelelfe he paft away,
    and loe, then was not hee;
  moreover I did feek for him,
    but found hee could not bee.
37 Take notice of the perfect man,
    and the upright attend:
  becaufe that unto fuch a man
    peace is his latter end.
38 But fuch men that tranfgreffors are
    together perifh fhall:
  the latter end fhall be cut off
    of the ungodly all,
39 But the falvation of the juft
    doth of Iehovah come:
  he is their ftrength to them in times
    that are moft troublefome.
40 Yea, help & free them will the Lord:
    he fhall deliver them
  from wiced men, becaufe that they
    doe put their truft in him.

Pfalme 38

A pfalme of David,
to bring to remembrance.

LORD, in thy wrath rebuke me not:
    nor in thy hot rage chaften mee.
2   Becaufe thine hand doth preffe me fore:
    and in me thy fhafts faftened bee.

3 There.

3 *There is* no soundnes in my flesh,
because thine anger I am in:
nor *is there* any rest within
my bones, by reason of my sin.

4 Because that mine iniquityes
ascended are above my head:
like as an heavy burden, they
to heavy upon me are layd.

5 My wounds stink, *and* corrupt they be:
my foolishnes doth make it so.

6 I troubled am, & much bow'd downe;
all the day long I mourning goe.

7 For with foule sores my loynes are fil'd:
& in my flesh *is* no soundnes.

8 I'me weak & broken sore; I roar'd
because of my hearts restlesnes.

9 All my desire's before thee, Lord;
nor is my groaning hid from thee.

10 My heart doth pant, my strength me fails:
& mine eye sight is gone from mee.

(2)

11 My freinds & lovers from my sore
stand off: off stand my kinsmen eke.

12 And they lay snares that seek my life,
that seek my hurt, they mischief speak,
And all day long imagin guile,

13 But as one deafe, I did not heare,
and as a dumb man I became
as if his mouth not open were.

14 Thus was I as man that heares not,
& in whose mouth reproofes none were.

15 becaufe

15 Becaufe o Lord, in thee I hope:
o Lord my God, thou wilt mee heare.

16 For fayd I, left or'e me they joy:
when my foot flips, they vaunt the more

17 themfelves 'gainft me. For I to halt
am neere, my grief's ftill mee before.

18 For my tranfgreffion I'le declare;
I for my fins will forry bee.

19 But yet my lively foes are ftrong,
who falfly hate me, multiplie.

20 Moreover they that doe repay
evill in ftead of good to mee,
becaufe I follow what is good,
to mee they adverfaryes bee.

21 Iehovah, doe not mee forfake:
my God o doe not farre depart

22 from mee. Make haft unto mine ayd,
o Lord who my falvation art.

Pfalme 39
To the chief mufician, even to Ieduthun,
a Pfalme of David.

I Sayd, I will look to my wayes,
left I fin with my tongue:
I'le keep my mouth with bit, while I
the wicked am among.

2 With filence tyed was my tongue,
my mouth I did refraine,
From fpeaking that thing which is good,
and ftirred was my paine.
Mine heart within me waxed hot.
while I was mufing long,

I inkindled

inkindled in me was the fire;
then spake I with my tongue.
4 Mine end, o Lord, & of my dayes
let mee the meafure learne;
that what a momentany thing
I am I may difcerne.
5 Behold thou mad'ft my dayes a fpan,
mine age as nought to thee:
furely each man at's beft eftate,
is wholly vanity.   Selah.
6 Sure in a vaine fhow walketh man;
fure ftir'd in vaine they are:
he heaps up riches,& kno's not
who fhall the fame gather.
(2)
7 And now, o Lord what wayt I for?
my hope is upon thee.
8 Free me from all my trefpaffes:
the fooles fcorne make not mee.
9 I was dumb nor opned my mouth,
this done becaufe thou haft.
10 Remove thy ftroke away fom mee:
by thy hands blow I waft.
11 When with rebukes thou doft correct
man for iniquity,.
thou blaft's his beauty like a moth:
fure each man 's vanity.   Selah.
12 Heare my pray'r, Lord, hark to my cry,
be not ftill at my tears:
for ftranger, & pilgrim with thee,
I 'me, as all my fathers.

13 O

13 O turne aſide a while from mee,
   that I may ſtrength recall:
before I doe depart from hence,
   and be noe more at all.

Pſalme 40.
To the chief muſician, a pſalme
of David.

WIth expectation for the Lord
    I wayted patiently,
and hee inclined unto mee.
   alſo he heard my cry.

2 He brought mee out of dreadfull-pit,
   out of the miery clay:
and ſet my feet upon a rock,
   hee ſtabliſhed my way.

3 And in my mouth put a new ſong,
   of prayſe our God uhto:
many ſhall ſee, & feare, upon
   the Lord ſhall truſt alſo.

4 Bleſt is the man that on the Lord
   maketh his truſt abide:
nor doth the proud reſpect, nor ſuch
   to lies as turne aſide.

5 O thou Iehovah, thou my God,
   haſt many a wonder wrought:
and likewiſe towards us thou haſt
   conceived many a thought.
Their ſumme cannot be reck'ned up'
   in order unto thee:
would I declare & ſpeak *of them,*
   beyond accounts they bee.

I 2   6 Thou

(2)

6 Thou facrifice & offering
   wouldſt not; thou boar'ſt mine eare:
burnt offring,& ſin offering
   thou neither didſt requere.

7 Then ſayd I: loe,I come: ith books
   rolle it is writt of mee.

8 To doe thy will,God, I delight:
   thy laws in my heart bee.

9 In the great congregation
   thy righteouſnes I ſhow:
loe,I have not refraynd my lips,
   Iehovah, thou doſt know.

10 I have not hid thy righteouſnes
   within my heart alone:
I have declar'd,thy faithfullnes
   and thy ſalvation:
Thy mercy nor thy truth have I
   from the great Church conceald.

11 Let not thy tender mercyes bee
   from mee o Lord with-held.
Let both thy kindnes & thy truth
   keep me my life throughout.

12 Becauſe innumerable ills
   have compaſt mee about:
My ſins have caught me ſo that I
   not able am to ſee:
more are they then hairs of my head,
   therefore my heart fails mee

(3)

13 Be pleaſ'd Lord, to deliver mee

to

to help me Lord make haſt.
14 At once abaſht & ſham'd let bee
　who ſeek my ſoule to waſte:
Let them be driven back,& ſham'd,
　that wiſh me miſery.
15 Let them be waſte, to quit their ſhame,
　that ſay to me,fy fy.
16 Let all be glad, & joy in thee,
　that ſeek thee: let them ſay
who thy ſalvation love, the Lord
　be magnifyde alway.
17 I both diſtreſt & needy am,
　the Lord yet thinks on mee:
my help & my deliverer thou
　my God, doe not tarry.

Pſalme 41
To the chief muſician, a pſalme
of David.

BLeſſed is hee that wiſely doth
　　unto the poore attend:
the Lord will him deliverance
　in time of trouble ſend.
2 Him God will keep, & make to live,
　on earth hee bleſt ſhall be,
nor doe thou him unto the will
　give of his enemie.
3 Vpon the bed of languiſhing,
　the Lord will ſtrengthen him:
thou alſo wilt make all his bed
　within his ſicknes time.
4 I ſayd, Iehouah, o be thou
I 3

merciful

mercifull unto mee;
  heale thou my foule, becaufe that I
    have finned againft thee.

5 Thofe men that be mine enemies,
  with evill mee defame:
  when will the time come hee fhall dye,
    and perifh fhall his name?

6 And if he come to fee *mee*, hee
  fpeaks vanity: his heart
  fin to it felfe heaps, when hee goes
    forth hee doth it impart.

(2)

7 All that me hate, againft mee they
  together whifper ftill:
  againft me they imagin doe
    to mee malicious ill.

8 *Thus doe they fay* fome ill difeafe,
  unto him cleaveth fore:
  and *feing now* he lyeth downe,
    he fhall rife up noe more.

9 Moreover my familiar freind,
  on whom my truft I fet,
  his heele againft mee lifted up,
    who of my bread did eat.

10 But Lord me pitty, & mee rayfe,
  that I may them requite.

11 By this I know affuredly,
  in mee thou doft delight:
  For o're mee triumphs not my foe.

12   And mee, thou doft mee ftay,
  in mine integrity; & fet'ft

mee

mee thee before for aye,

23 Bleſt hath Iehovah Iſraels God
from everlaſting *been*,
alſo unto everlaſting:
Amen, yea and Amen.

THE

SECOND BOOKE.

PSALME 42

To the chief muſician, *Maſchil*, for the
Sonnes of Korah.

Like as the Hart panting doth bray
after the water brooks,
even in ſuch wiſe o God, my ſoule,
after thee panting looks.

2 For God, even for the liuing God,
my ſoule it thirſteth ſore:
oh when ſhall I come & appeare,
the face of God before.

3 My teares have been unto mee meat,
by night alſo by day,
while all the day they unto mee
where is thy God doe ſay.

4 When as I doe in minde record
theſe things, then me upon
I doe my ſoule out poure, for I
with multitude had gone:
With them unto Gods houſe I went,
with voyce of joy & prayſe:

I *with*

PSALM xlii.

I with a multitude did goe
  that did keepe-holy-days.
5 My foule why art caft downe?& art
  ftirr'd in mee: thy hope place
in God, for yet him prayfe I fhall
  for the help of his face.

(2)

6 My God, my foule in mee's caft downe,
  therefore thee minde I will
from Iordanes & Hermonites land,
  and from the litle hill.
7 At the noyfe of thy water fpouts
  deep unto deep doth call:
thy waves they are gone over mee,
  alfo thy billowes all.
8 His loving kindnes yet the Lord
  command will in the day:
and in the night his fong with mee,
  to my lifes God I'le pray.
9 I unto God will fay, my Rock
  why haft thou forgot mee?
why goe I fad, by reafon of
  preffure of th' enemie.
10 As with a fword within my bones
  my foes reproach mee do:
while all the day, where is thy God?
  they doe fay mee unto.
11 My foule o wherefore doft thou bowe
  thy felfe downe heavily;
and wherefore in mee makeft thou
  a ftirr tumultuoufly?

Hope

Hope thou in God, becaufe I fhall
   with prayfe him yet advance:
who is my God, alfo he is
   health of my countenance.

Pfalme 43.

IVdge me, o God, & plead my caufe
   from nation mercyleffe;
from the guilefull & man unjuft,
   o fend thou me redreffe.

2 For of my ftrength thou art the God,
   why caft's thou mee thee fro:
why goe I mourning for the fore
   oppreffion of the foe?

3 Thy light o fend out & thy truth,
   let them lead, & bring mee,
unto thy holy hill, & where
   thy tabernacles bee.

4 Then will I to Gods Altar goe,
   to God my joyes gladnes:
upon the Harp o God my God
   I will thy prayfe expreffe.

5 My foule o wherfore doft thou bowe
   thy felfe downe heavily;
and wherefore in mee makeft thou
   a ftirre tumultuoufly?
Hope thou in God, becaufe I fhall
   with prayfe him yet advance:
who is my God, alfo he is
   health of my countenance.

Pfalme 44

To the chief mufician, for the fonnes-
of Korah.   K   PSAL.

PSALM xliv.

WEE with our eares have heard, o God,
    our fathers have us told,
what works thou diddeſt in their dayes;
    in former dayes of old.
2 *How* thy hand drave the heathen out,
    and them thou planted haſt;
how thou the people didſt afflict,
    and thou didſt them out-caſt.
3 For they got not by their owne ſword
    the lands poſſeſſion,
neither yet was it their owne arme
    wrought their ſalvation:
But thy right hand, thine arme alſo,
    thy countenances light;
becauſe that of thine owne good will
    thou didſt in them delight.
4 Thou art my king, o mighty God,
    thou doſt the ſame indure:
doe thou for Iacob by command
    deliverances procure.
5 Through thee as with a horne wee will
    puſh downe our enemies:
through thy name will wee tread them downe
    that up againſt us riſe.
6 Becauſe that I will in no wiſe
    any affiance have,
upon my bow, neither is it
    my ſword that ſhall mee ſave.
7 But from our enemies us thou ſav'd,
    and put our foes to ſhame.
8 In God wee boaſt all the day long,

and

74

and for aye prayſe thy name.   Selah.

(2)

9 But thou haſt caſt us off away,
   thou makeſt us alſo
to be aſham'd; neither doſt thou
   forth with our armies goe.

10 Vs from before the enemy
   thou makeſt back recoyle:
likewiſe they which our haters bee,
   for themſelves us doe ſpoyle.

11 Thou haſt us given like to ſheep
   to ſlaughter *that belong*:
alſo thou haſt us ſcattered
   the heathen folk among.

12 Thou doſt thy people ſet to ſale
   whereby no wealth doth riſe:
neither doſt thou obtaine increaſe
   of riches by their price.

13 Vnto our neighbours a reproach
   thou doeſt us expoſe,
a ſcorne we are & mocking ſtock,
   to them that us incloſe.

14 Among the heathen people thou
   a by word doſt us make:
alſo among the nations,
   at us their heads they ſhake.

15 Before me my confuſion
   it is continually,
and of my countenance the ſhame
   hath over covered mee.

16 Becauſe of his voyce that doth ſcorne,

K 2   and

and scoffingly despight:
by reason of the enemy,
   and selfe revenging wight.

(3)

17 All this is come on us, wee yet
  have not forgotten thee:
neither against thy covenant
  have wee dealt faithleslie.

18 Our heart is not turn'd back, nor have
  our steps from thy way stray'd;

19 Though us thou brake in dragons place,
  and hid us in deaths shade.

20 had wee forgot Gods name, or stretcht
  to a strange God our hands:

21 Shall not God search this out? for hee
  hearts secrets understands.

22 Yea, for thee all day wee are kil'd:
  counted as sheep to slay.

23 Awake, why sleepst thou, Lord? arise,
  cast us not off for aye.

24 Thy countenance away from us
  o wherefore dost thou hide?
of our grief & oppression
  forgetfull dost abide.

25 For our soule is bowd downe to dust:
  to earth cleaves our belly.

25 Rise for our help, & us redeeme,
  because of thy mercy.

Psalme 45

To the chief musician upon Shoshannim, for-
the sonnes of Korab, Maschil a song of loves.

PSAL-

PSALME xlv.

MY heart good mater boyleth forth,
    my works touching the King
I speak: my tongue is as the pen
    of Scribe swiftly writing.
2 Fairer thou art then sonnes of men,
    grace in thy lips is shed:
because of this the Lord hath thee
    for evermore blessed.
3 Thy wasting sword o mighty one
    gird thou upon thy thigh:
thy glorious-magnificence,
    and comely majesty.
4 Ride forth upon the word of truth,
    meeknes & righteousnes:
and thy right hand shall lead thee forth
    in works of dreadfulnes.
5 Within the heart of the kings foes
    thine arrows piercing bee:
whereby the people overcome,
    shall fall downe under thee.
6 Thy throne o God, for ever is,
    the scepter of thy state
7 right scepter is. Iustice thou lov'st,
    but wickednes dost hate:
Because of this, God ev'n thy God
    hee hath annoynted thee,
with oyle of gladnes above them,
    that thy companions bee.
8 Myrrhs, Aloes, and Cassias *smell*,
    all of thy garments *had*:
out of the yvory pallaces

K 3   **they**

wherby they made thee glad.

9 Amongst thine honourable maids
    kings daughters present were,
the Queen is set at thy right hand
    in fine gold of Ophir.

(2)

10 Harken o daughter, & behold,
    doe thou incline thine eare:
doe thou forget thine owne people,
    and house of thy father.

11 So shall the king delighting-rest
    himselfe in thy beautie:
and bowing downe worship thou him,
    because thy Lord is hee.

12 Then shall be present with a gift
    the daughter there of Tyre:
the wealthy ones of the people
    thy favour shall desire.

13 The daughter of the king she is,
    all glorious within:
.and with imbroderies of gold,
    her garments wrought have been.

14 She is led in unto the king.
    in robes with needle wrought:
the virgins that doe follow her
    shall unto thee be brought.

15 They shall be brought forth with gladnes,
    also with rejoycing,
so shall they entrance have into
    the Pallace of the king.

16 Thy children shall in stead of those
    that were thy fathers bee: whom

whom thou mayſt place in all the earth
in princely diginty.

27 Thy name remembred I will make
through generations all:
therefore for ever & for aye
the people prayſe thee ſhall.

Pſalme 46

To the chief muſician, for the ſonnes of
Korah, a ſong upon Alemoth.

GOD is our refuge, ſtrength, & help
in troubles very neere.

2 Therefore we will not be afrayd,
though th'earth removed were.
Though mountaines move to midſt of ſeas

3 Though waters roaring make
and troubled be, at whoſe ſwellings
although the mountaines ſhake.　　Selah.

4 There is a river ſtreames whereof
ſhall rejoyce Gods city:
the holy place the tent wherin
abideth the moſt high.

5 God is within the midſt of her,
moved ſhee ſhall not bee:
God ſhall be unto her an help,
in the morning early.

6 The nations made tumultuous noyſe,
the kingdomes moved were:
he did give forth his thundering voyce
the earth did melt *with feare*.

7 The God of Armies is with us
ih'eternall Iehovah:

the

the God of Iacob is for us
    a refuge high. Selah.
8 O come yee forth behold the works
    which Iehovah hath wrought,
the fearfull defolations,
    which on the earth he brought.
9 Vnto the utmoft ends of th'earth
    warres into peace hee turnes:
the fpeare he cuts, the bowe he breaks,
    in fire the chariots burnes.
10 Be ftill, & know that I am God,
    exalted be will I
among the heathen: through the earth
    I 'le be exalted hye.
11 The God of armyes is with us,
    th'eternall Iehovah:
the God of Iacob is for us
    a refuge high. Selah.

Pfalme 47.

To the chief mufician: a pfalme for the
Sonnes of Korah.

CLap hands all people, fhrout for joy,
    to God with voyce of finging mirth:
2 For high Iehovah fearfull is,
    a great King over all the earth.
3   People to us he doth fubdue,
    and nations under our feet lay.
4 For us our heritage he chofe,
    his deare Iacobs glory. Selah.
5   God is afcended with a fhout:
    Iehovah with the trumpets noyfe.

6 Sing

6　Sing pſalmes to God, ſing pſalmes, ſing
　　unto our King with ſinging voyce.　(pſalmes
7　　For God is King of all the earth,
　　ſing yee pſalmes of inſtruction:
8　Over the heathen God will reigne
　　God ſits his holy throne upon.
9　　To the people of Abrahams-God
　　Princes of peoples gathered bee,
　　for ſhields of th'earth to God belong:
　　he is exalted mightylie.

Pſalme 48
To the chief muſician, a ſong & pſalme for
the ſonnes of Korah.

GReat is Iehovah, & he is
　to be prayſed greatly
within the city of our God,
　in his mountaine holy.
2　For ſituation beautifull,
　　the joy of the whole earth
　mount Sion; the great Kings city
　　on the ſides of the north.
3　God in her pallaces is knowne
　　to be a refuge high.
4　For loe, the kings aſſembled were:
　　they paſt together by.
5　They ſaw, & ſo they merveiled,
　　were troubled, fled for feare.
6　Trembling ſeiz'd on them there & paine
　　like her that childe doth beare.
7　The navies that of Tarſhiſh are
　　in pieces thou breakeſt:

L　　　　　　　　　　even

ev'n with a very blaſt of winde
  coming out of the eaſt.
8 As we heard, ſo we ſaw within
  the Lord of hoaſts citty,
in our Gods citty, God will it
  ſtabliſh eternally.   Selah.

(2)

9 O God we have had thoughts upon
  thy free benignity,
within the very midle part
  of thy temple holy,
10 According to thy name, o God
  ſo is thy prayſe unto
the ends of earth: thy right hand 's full
  of righteouſnes alſo.
11 Let the mountaine Sion rejoyce,
  and triumph let them make
who are the daughters of Iudah,
  ev'n for thy judgements ſake.
12 About the hill of Sion walk,
  and goe about her yee,
and doe yee reckon up thereof
  the tow'rs *that therein* bee.
13 Doe yee full well her bulwarks mark,
  her Pallaces view well,
that to the generation
  to come yee may it tell.
14 For this ſame God he is our God
  for ever & for aye:
likewiſe unto the very death
  he guides us in our way.

PSALM

Pſalme 49
To the chief muſician a pſalme for the
ſonnes of Korah.

HEare this all people, all give eare
that dwell the world all o're.
2 Sonnes both of low, & higher men,
joyntly both rich & poore.
3 My mouth it ſhall variety
of wiſdome be ſpeaking:
and my hearts meditation ſhall
be of underſtanding.
4 Vnto a ſpeech proverbiall
I will mine eare incline;
I will alſo upon the Harp
open my dark doctrine.
5 Why ſhould I be at all afrayd
in dayes that evill bee:
when that my heeles iniquity
about ſhall compaſſe mee.

(2)

6 Thoſe men that make their great eſtates.
their ſtay to truſt unto,
who in the plenty of their wealth
themſelves doe boaſt alſo:
7 Ther 's not a man *of them* that can
by any meanes redeeme
his brother, nor give unto God
enough to ranſome him.
8 So deare their ſoules redemption is
& ever ceaſeth it.

L 2   9 That

9 That he should still for ever live
  and never see the pit.
10 For he doth see that wise man dye,
  the foole and brutish too
  to perish, & their rich estate
  to others leave they doo.
11 They think their houses are for aye
  to generations all
  their dwelling places, & their lands
  by their owne names they call.
12 Neverthelesse, in honour man,
  abideth not a night:
  become he is just like unto
  the beasts that perish quite.
13 This their owne way their folly is;
  yet whatsoe're they say,
  their successors that follow them
  doe well approve. Selah.
14 Like sheep so are they layd in grave,
  death shall them feed upon;
  & th'upright over them in morn
  shall have dominion.
  And from the place where they doe dwell,
  the beauty which they have,
  shall utterly consume away
  in the devouring grave.

(3)
15 But surely God redemption
  unto my soule will give,
  even from the power of the grave,
  for he will me receive.   Selah.

16 Be

16 Be not afrayd when as a man
    in wealth is made to grow,
and when the glory of his house
    abundantly doth flow.

17 Becaufe he fhall carry away
    nothing when he doth dye:
neither fhall after him defcend
    ought of his dignity.

18 And albeit that he his foule
    in time of his life bleft,
and men will prayfe thee, when as thou
    much of thy felfe makeft.

19 He fhall goe to his fathers race,
    they never fhall fee light.

20 Man in honour, & know'th not, is
    like beafts that perifh quite.

Pfalme 50.
A pfalme of Afaph.

THe mighty God, the Lord hath fpoke,
    and he the earth doth call,
from the uprifing of the Sun,
    thereof unto the fall.

2 The mighty God hath clearely fhyn'd
    out of the mount Sion,
which is of beauty excellent
    the full perfection.

3 Our God fhall come, and not be ftill
    fire fhall wafte in his fight;
and round about him fhall be rayf'd
    a ftorme of vehement might.

4 His folk to judge he from above

L 3

calls

85

calls heavens,& earth likewife,
5 Bring mee my Saints,that cov'nant make
with mee by facrifice.
6 And the heavens fhall his righteoufnes
fhew forth apparentlie:
becaufe the mighty God himfelfe
a righteous judge will bee.   Selah.
(2)
7 Heare, o my people,& I will
fpeake,I will teftify
alfo to thee o Ifraell,
I even thy God am I.
8 As for thy facrifices I
will finde no fault with thee,
or thy burnt offrings,*which have been*
at all times before mee.
9 Ile take no bullocks,nor he-goates
from houfe,or.foldes of thine.
10 For forreft beafts,& cattell all
on thoufand hills are mine.
11 The flying foules of the mountaines
all of them doe I know:
and every wilde beaft of the field
it.is with mee alfo.
12 If I were hungry I would not
it unto thee declare:
for mine the habitable world,
and fullnes of it *are*.
13 Of bullocks eate the flefh,or drink
the blood of goates will I ?
14 Thanks offer unto God,& pay

thy

thy vowes to the moſt high.
15 And in the day of trouble ſore
doe thou unto mee cry,
and I will thee deliver, and
thou mee ſhalt glorify.

(3)

16 But to the wicked God ſayth, why
doſt thou the mention make
of my ſtatutes, why in thy mouth
ſhould'ſt thou my cov'nant take?
17 Sith thou doſt hate teaching and doſt
my words behinde thee caſt
18 When thou didſt ſee a thief, then thou
with him conſented haſt;
And likewiſe with adulterers
thy part hath been the ſame.
19 Thy mouth to evill thou doſt give,
and guile thy tongue doth frame;
Thou ſitteſt, thou doſt ſpeake againſt
the man that is thy brother:
and thou doſt ſlaunder him that is
the ſonne of thine owne mother.
21 Theſe things haſt thou committed, and
in ſilence I kept cloſe:
that I was altogether like
thy ſelfe, thou didſt ſuppoſe:
I'le thee reprove, & in order
before thine eyes them ſet.
22 O therefore now conſider this
yee that doe God forget:
Leſt I you teare, & there be no

any

any deliverer.

23 He glorifieth mee that doth
    prayse unto mee offer.
24 And hee that doth order *aright*
    his conversation,
  to him will I give that hee may
    see Gods salvation.

Psalme 51.

To the chief musician, a psalme of David, when
Nathan the prophet came unto him, after he
had gone in unto Bathsheba.

HAve mercy upon mee o God,
  in thy loving kyndnes:
in multitude of thy mercyes
    blot out my trespasses.

2 From mine iniquity doe thou
    wash mee most perfectly
and also from this sin of mine
    doe thou mee purify.

3 Because, of my transgressions
    my selfe doe take notice,
and sin that I committed have
    before mee ever is.

4 Gainst thee, thee only I have sin'd
    this ill done thee before:
when thou speakst just thou art, & cleare
    when thou dost judge therfore.

5 Behold, how in iniquity
    I did my shape receive:
also my mother *that mee bare*
    in sin did mee conceive.

6 Behold

6 Behold,thou doſt deſire the truth
   within the inward part:
and thou ſhalt make mee wiſdome know
   in ſecret of my heart.

7 With hyſope doe me purify,
   I ſhall be cleanſed ſo:
doe thou mee waſh,& then I ſhall
   be whiter then the ſnow.

8 Of joy & of gladnes doe thou
   make me to heare the voyce:
that ſo the bones which thou haſt broke
   may cheerfully rejoyce.

9 From the beholding of my ſin
   hide thou away thy face:
alſo all mine iniquityes
   doe utterly deface.

(2)

10 A cleane heart(Lord)in me create,
   alſo a ſpirit right

11 in me renew. O caſt not mee
   away out of thy ſight;
Nor from me take thy holy ſpirit.

12 Reſtore the joy to mee
  of thy ſalvation,& uphold
   me with thy ſpirit free.

13 Then will I teach thy wayes to thoſe
   that work iniquitie:
and by this meanes ſhall ſinners bee
  converted unto thee.

14 O God, God of my health, ſet mee
  free from bloud guiltines,

M

and

and so my tongue shall joyfully.
sing of thy righteousnes.

15 O Lord-my-stay, let thou my lips
by thee be opened,
and by my mouth thy prayses shall
be openly shewed.

16 For thou desir'st not sacrifice,
it would I freely bring:
neither dost thou contentment take
in a whole burnt offring.

17 The sacrifices of the Lord
they are a broken sprite:
God, thou wilt not despise a heart
that's broken, & contrite.

18 In thy good pleasure o doe thou
doe good to Sion hill:
the walles of thy Ierusalem
o doe thou build up still.

19 The sacrifice of justice shall
please thee. with burnt offring,
and whole burnt offring; then they shall
calves to thine Altar bring.

Another of the same.

O GOD, have mercy upon mee,
according to thy kindenes deare:
and as thy mercyes many bee,
quite doe thou my transgressions cleare.

2   From my perversnes mee wash through,
and from my sin mee purify.

3 For my transgressions I doe know,

before

before mee is my sin dayly.

4 Gainst thee,thee only sin'd have I,
& done this evill in thy sight:
that when thou speakst thee justify
men may,and judging cleare thee quite.

5 Loe,in injustice shape't I was:
in sin my mother conceav'd mee.

6 Loe,thou in th'inwards truth lov'd haz:
and made mee wise in secrecie.

7 Purge me with hyssope,& I cleare
shall be;mee wash,& then the snow

8 I shall be whiter. Make me heare
Ioy & gladnes, the bones which so
Thou broken hast joy cheerly shall.

9 Hyde from my sins thy face away
blot thou iniquityes out all
which are upon mee any way.

(2)

10 Create in mee cleane heart *at last*
God: a right spirit in me new make.

11 Nor from thy presence quite me cast,
thy holy spright nor from me take.

12 Mee thy salvations joy restore,
and stay me with thy spirit free.

13 I wil, transgressors teach thy lore,
and sinners shall be turnd to thee.

14 Deliver mee from guilt of bloud,
o God, God of my health-saving,
which if thou shalt vouchsafe,aloud
thy righteousnes my tongue shall sing.

15 My lips doe thou,o Lord,unclose,

M 2

and

and thy prayſe ſhall my mouth forth ſhowe
16 For ſacrifice thou haſt not choſe,
that I ſhould it on thee beſtow:
Thou joy'ſt not in burnt ſacrifice.
17 Gods ſacrifices are a ſp'ryte
broken; o God,thou'lt not deſpiſe,
a heart that's broken & contrite.
18 In thy good will doe thou beſtow
on Sion goodnes bounteouſlie:
Ieruſalems walles that lye ſo low·
doe thou vouchſafe to edifie.
19 Then ſhalt thou pleaſe to entertaine
the ſacrifices with content
of righteouſnes, the offrings ſlaine,
which unto thee wee ſhall preſent,
Together with the offerings
ſuch as in fire whole burned are:
and then they ſhall their bullocks bring,
offrings to be on thine altar.

Pſalme 52

To the chief muſician, ◌Maſchil. a pſalme of
David:when Doeg the Edomite came and
told Saule, & ſayd unto him, Dauid is
come to the houſe of Ahimilech.

O Man of might, wherefore doſt thou
thus boaſt thy ſelfe in ill?
the goodnes of the mighty God
endureth ever ſtill.
2 Thy tongue preſumptuouſly doth
miſchievous things deviſe:
it is like to a razor ſharp,

working

working deceitfull lies.

3 Thou lovest evil more then good,
   more to speak lies then right.
4 O guilefull tongue,thou dost in all
   devouring words delight.
5 God shall likewise for evermore
   destroying thee deface,
he shall take thee away,& pluck
   thee from thy dwelling place,
And also root thee out from off
   the land of the living.   Selah.
6 The righteous also shall it see
   and feare, at him laughing.
7 Loe,this the man *that* made not God
   his strength: but trusted in
his store of wealth,himselfe made strong
   in his mischievous sin.
8 But in the house of God *am* I
   like a greene Olive-tree:
I trust for ever & for aye,
   in Gods benignitie.
9 Thee will I prayse for evermore,
   because thou hast done this:
and I'le wayt on thy name, for good
   before thy Saints that is.

Psalme 53.

To the chief musician upon Mahalath,
   Maschil.a *psalme* of David.

THe foole in's heart saith,*there's* no God;
   they are corrupt,have done
abominable practises;

        M 3   that

that doth good there is none.

2 The Lord from heaven looked downe
    on sonnes of men, to see
if any that doth understand,
    that seeketh God there bee.

3 All are gone back,together they
    ev'n filthy are become:
and there is none that doeth good,
    noe not so much as one.

4 The workers of iniquityes
    have they noe knowledge all?
who eate my people: they eate bread,
    and on God doe not call.

5 Greatly they fear'd,*where* noe feare was,
    'gainst thee in camp that lyes
his bones God scattered,& them sham'd
    for God doth *them* despise.

6 Who Israells health from Sion gives?
    his folks captivitie
when God shall turne: Iacob shall joye
    glad Israell shall bee.

Psalme 54

To the chief musician on Neginoth, Maschil,*a*
psalm: of David, when the Ziphims came & sayd
to Saul, doth not David hide himselfe with us?

PReserve mee, by thy name, o God,
    & by thy strength judge mee.

2 O God, my pray'r heare, give eare to
    words in my mouth that bee.

3 For strangers up against me rise,
    and who oppresse me sore,

                      purfue

purſue my ſoule, neither have they
   ſet God themſelves before.   Selah.

4 Loe, God helps mee, the Lord's with them
   that doe my ſoule ſuſtaine.

5 He ſhall reward ill to my foes:
   them in thy truth reſtrayne.

6 Vnto thee ſacrifice will I,
   with voluntarines,
  Lord, to thy name I will give prayſe,
   becauſe of thy goodnes.

7 For he hath mee delivered,
   out of all miſeryes:
  and its deſire mine eye hath ſeen
   upon mine enemyes.

Pſalme 55

To the chief muſician on Neginoth, Maſchil,
   a pſalme of David.

O GOD, doe thou give eare unto
   my ſupplication:
and doe not hide thy ſelfe away
   from my petition,

2 Bee thou attentive unto mee,
   and anſwer mee returne,
  I in my meditation
   doe make a noyſe & mourne.

3 Becauſe of th'enemies voyce, becauſe
   the wicked haue oppreſt,
  for they injuſtice on mee caſt
   and in wrath mee deteſt.

4 My heart in mee is payn'd, on mee
   deaths terrors fallen bee,

                       5 Trembling

5 Trembling & feare are on mee come,
   horrour hath covered mee.
6 Then did I say, o who to mee
   wings of a dove will give;
   that I might flie away & might
   in quiet dwelling live.
7 Loe, I would wander farre away,
   and in the desart rest.   Selah,
8 Soone would I scape from windy storme,
   from violent tempest.

(2)

9 Lord bring on them destruction,
   doe thou their tongues divide;
   for strife & violence I within
   the city have espy'd.
10 About it on the walles thereof,
   they doe walk night & day:
   mischief also & sorrow doe
   in middest of it stay.
11 In midst thereof there's wickednes;
   deceitfullnes also,
   and out of the broad streets thereof
   guilefullnes doth not go.
12 For t'was no foe reproacht mee, then
   could I have borne; nor did
   my foe against me lift himselfe
   from him had I me hid.
13 But thou it was, the man that wert
   my well esteemed peere,
   which wast to mee my speciall guide,
   and mine acquaintance neere.

84 wee

96

14 Wee did together counſell take
   in ſweet ſociety:
and wee did walk into the houſe
   of God in company.
15 Let death ſeize on them,& let them
   goe downe quick into hell:
for wickednes among them is
   in places where they dwell.

(2)

16 As for mee, I will call on God;
   and mee the Lord ſave ſhall.
17 Ev'ning morn,& at noon will I
   pray, & aloud will call,
18 and he ſhall heare my voyce. He hath
   in peace my ſoule ſet free
from warre that was 'gainſt mee,becauſe
   there many were with mee.
19 God ſhall heare,& them ſmite,ev'n he
   that doth of old abide;   Selah.
becauſe they have no change,therefore
   Gods feare they lay aſide.
20 Gainſt ſuch as be at peace with him
   hee hath put forth his hand:
he hath alſo the covenant
   which he had made prophan'd.
21 His words then butter ſmoother were,
   but warre in's heart:his words
more then the oyle were ſoftened
   but yet they were drawne ſwords.
22 Thy burden caſt upon the Lord,
   and he ſuſtaine thee ſhall:

N   nor

nor shall he suffer righteous ones
to be remov'd at all.
23 But thou o God, shalt downe to hell
bring them who bloody bee,
guilefull shall not live halfe their dayes:
but I will trust in thee.

Psalme 56.

To the chief musician upo Ionath Elem Recho-
-kim, Michtam of David, when the Philistims
tooke him in Gath.

LORD, pitty mee, becaufe
man would up swallow mee:
and fighting all the day throughout,
oppresse mee sore doth hee.
2 Mine enemies they would
me swallow up dayly;
for they be many that doe fight
against mee, o most high.
3 I'le put my trust in thee,
what time I am afrayd.
4 In God I'le prayse his word, in God
my confidence have stayd;
I will not be afrayd
what flesh can doe to mee.
5 All day they wrest my words: their thoughts
for ill against me bee.
6 They joyne themseves together;
themselves they closely hyde;
they mark my steps when for my soule
wayting they doe abyde.
7 Shall they make an escape

be

by their iniquity;
thou in thine anger downe depreſſe
the folk, o God mighty.
8 My wandrings thou doſt tell,.
put thou my weeping teares
into thy bottle: *are* they not
within thy regiſters.
9 Then ſhall my foes turne back,
when I crye unto thee:
this I doe know aſſuredly,
becauſe God is for mee.
10 In God I'le prayſe his word:
the Lords word I will prayſe.
11 In God I truſt: I will not feare
what man 'gainſt mee can rayſe.
12 Thy vowes on me o God;
I'le render prayſe to thee.
13 Becauſe that thou my ſoule from death
delivering doſt free;
Deliver wilt not thou
my feet from downe falling?
ſo that I may walk before God
ith light of the living.

Pſalme 57

To the chief muſician Altaſchith, Michtam of
David, when he fled from Saul in the cave.

O GOD, to me be mercifull,
be mercifull to mee:
becauſe my ſoule for ſhelter-ſafe
betakes it ſelfe to thee.
Yea in the ſhaddow of thy wings,
my refuge I have plac't,   N 2   until

untill the fe fore calamities
    fhall quite be over paft.
2 To God moft high I cry:the God
    that doth for me performe.
3 He will from heaven fend, & fave
    mee from the fpightfull fcorne
Of him that would with greedy haft,
    fwallow me vtterly: Selah.
the Lord from heaven will fend forth
    his grace & verity.
4 My foule's 'mongft lions, & I lye
    with men on-fier-fet:
mens fonnes whofe teeth are fpears,& fhafts.
    whofe tongues as fwords are whet.
5 O God,doe thou exalt thy felfe,
    above the heavens high:
up over all the earth alfo
    lifted be thy glory.
6 They for my fteps prepar'd a net,
    my foule is bow'd; a pit
they dig'd before me, but *themfelves*
    are fall'n in midft of it.   Selah.
7 My heart o God, prepared is,
    prepared is my heart,
fing will I, & fing prayfe with pfalmes.
8   Vp o my glorie ftart;
Wake Pfaltery & Harp, I will
    awake in the morning.
9 Among the folk I 'le prayfe thee,Lord,
    'mongft nations to thee fing.

10 Fo

10 For great unto the heavens is
  thy mercifull bounty:
thy verity alſo doth reach
  unto the cloudy ſkye.
11 O God, doe thou exalt thy ſelfe,
  above the heavens high:
up over all the earth alſo
  lifted *be* thy glory.

Pſalme 58
To the chief muſician, Altaſchi.h,
  michtam of David.

DOe yee o congregation,
  indeed ſpeak righteouſnes?
and o yee ſons of earthly men,
  doe yee judge uprightnes?
2 Yea you in heart will working be
  injurious-wickednes;
and in the land you will weigh out
  your hands violentnes.
3 The wicked are eſtranged from
  the womb, they goe aſtray
as ſoone as ever they are borne;
  uttering lyes are they.
4 Their poyſon's like ſerpents poyſon:
  they like deafe Aſpe, her eare
5 that ſtops. Though Charmer wiſely charme,
  his voice ſhe will not heare.
6 Within their mouth doe thou their teeth
  break out, o God moſt ſtrong,
doe thou Iehovah, the great teeth
  break of the lions young.

N 3   7 As

7 As waters let them melt away,
    that run continually:
and when he bends his shafts, let them
    as cut asunder bee.

8 Like to a snayle that melts, so let
    each of them passe away;
like to a womans untimely birth
    see Sun that neuer they may.

9 Before your potts can feele the thornes,
    take them away shall hee,
as with a whirlwinde both living,
    and in his jealousee.

10 The righteous will rejoyce when as
    the vengeance he doth see:
his feet wash shall he in the blood
    of them that wicked bee.

11 So that a man shall say, surely
    for righteous there is fruit:
sure there's a God that in the earth
    judgement doth execute.

Psalme 59

To the chief musician Altaschith, Michtam of
  David: when Saul sent, & they watched the
    house to kill him.

O GOD from them deliver mee
    that are mine enemies:
set thou me up on high from them
    that up against me rise.

2 Deliver mee from them that work
    grievous-iniquity:
and be a saviour unto mee.

from

PSALME lix.

from men that be bloody.

3 For loe,they for my foule lay wayt,
    the ftrong cauffeffe combine
againft me,not for my crime,Lord,
    nor any fin of mine.

4 Without iniquity in me
    they run, & ready make
themfelves,doe thou behold,alfo
    unto my help awake.

5 Lord God of hoaft,thou Ifraels God,
    rife to vifit therefore
all heathens;who fin wilfully,
    to them fhew grace no more.

6 At ev'ning they returne;& like
    to dogs a noyfe doe make;
and fo about the city round
    a compaffe they doe take.

7 Behold they belch out with their mouths,
    within their lips fwords are:
for who is he (doe thefe men fay)
    which *us* at all doth heare.

8 But thou o *Lord*,at them wilt laugh,
    and heathens all wilt mock.

9 *And for* his ftrength, I'le wayt on thee
    for God is my high Rock.

(2)

10 God of my mercy manyfold
    with good fhall prevent mee:
and my defire upon my foes
    the Lord will let mee fee.

11 Slay them not,left my folk forget:

but

but scatter them abroad
by thy strong-power, & bring them downe,
who art our shield o God.

12 For their mouths sin,& their lips words,
and in their pride them take:
and for their cursing,& lying
which in their speech they make.

13 Consume in wrath, consume & let
them be no more;that they
may know that God in Iacob rules,
to th'ends of th'earth. Selah.

14 And at ev'ning let them returne,
and like dogs a noyse make;
and so about the citty round
a compasse let them take.

15 And let them wander up & downe
seeking what they may eat,
and if they be not satiffiyde,
then let them grudge thereat,

16 But I will sing thy powre,& shout
i'th morning thy kindeneffe:
for thou my towre & refuge art
in day of my diftreffe.

17 Thou art my strength,& unto thee,
sing psalmes of prayse will I:
for God is mine high towre, he is
the God of my mercy.

Psalme 60.

To the chief musician upon Shushan Eduth
Michta n of David,to teach. when he strove with
Aram Naharaim, & with Aram Zobah when

Ioab

PSALME lx.

Ioab returned,& fmote of Edom in the valley
of falt, twelve thoufand.

O GOD,thou haft rejected us,
and fcattered us abroad:
thou haft difpleafed been with us,
returne to us o God.

2 The land to tremble thou haft cauf'd,
thou it afunder brake:
doe thou the breaches of it heale,
for it doth moveing fhake.

3 Thou haft unto thy people fhew'd
things that are hard,thou haft
alfo the cup of trembleing
given to them to taft.

4 But unto them that doe thee feare
a Banner to difplay
thou given haft to be lift up
for thy truths fake.Selah.

5 That thofe who thy beloved are
delivered may bee,
o doe thou fave with thy right hand,
and anfwer give to mee.

6 God in his holynes hath fpoke,
rejoyce therein will I,
Shechem I will divide,& meete
of Succoth the valley.

7 To mee doth Gilead appertaine,
Manaffeh mine befides:
Ephraim the ftrength is of my head,
Iudah my lawes prefcribes.

8 Moab's my wafh-por, I will caft
O

over

over Edom my fhoo,
o Paleftine, becaufe of mee
be thou triumphant too.

9 O who is it that will mee lead
to th'citty fortifyde?
and who is he that will become
into Edom my guide?

10 Is it not thou,o God,who hadft
caft us off heretofore?
and thou o God,who with our hoafts
wouldft not goe out before?

11 O give to us help from diftreffe
for mans help is but vaine:

12 Through God wee'l doe great acts,he fhall
our foes tread with difdaine.

Pfalme 61

To the chief mufician upon Neginath,
A pfalme of David.

HArken o God, unto my cry,
unto my prayr attend.

2 When my heart is oppreft, I'le cry
to thee from the earths end.
Doe thou mee lead unto the rock
that higher is then I.

3 For thou my hiding-place, haft been
ftrong Fort from th'enemy.

4 Within thy Tabernacle I
for ever will abide,
wi hin the covert of thy wings
I'le feek my felfe to hide.   Selah

5 For thou o God,haft heard the vowes

that

that I to thee have paſt:
their heritage that feare thy name;
to mee thou given haſt.
6 ' Thou to the dayes of the Kings life;
wilt make addition:
his yeares as generation,
and generation.
7 Before the face of the ſtrong God
he ſhall abide for aye:
doe thou mercy & truth prepare
that him preſerve they may.
8 So then I will unto thy name
ſing prayſe perpetually,
that I the vowes which I have made
may pay continually.

Pſalme 62

To the chief muſician, to Ieduthun,
a pſalme of David.

TRuly my ſoule in ſilence waytes
the mighty God upon:
from him it is that there doth come
all my ſalvation.
2 He only is my rock, & my
ſalvation; it is hee
that my defence is, ſo that I
mov'd greatly ſhall not bee.
3 How long will yee miſchief deviſe
'gainſt man; be ſlaine yee ſhall,
all yee are as a tottring fence,
& like a bowing wall.
4 Yet they conſult to caſt him downe

O 2

from.

from his excellency:
lyes they doe love,with mouth they bleffe,
 but they curfe inwardly. Selah.
5 Yet thou my foule in filent wayt
 the mighty God upon:
becaufe from him there doth arife
 my expectation.
6 He only is my rock,& my
 falvation, it is hee
that my defence is, fo that I
 fhall never mooved bee.
7 In God is my falvation,
 alfo is my glory:
and the rock of my fortitude,
 my hope in God doth ly.
8 Yee people,fee that you on him
 doe put your truft alway,
before him poure ye out your hearts:
 God is our hopefull-ftay. Selah.
9 Surely meane men are vanity
 high mens fonnes are a lye:
in ballance laid together are
 lighter then vanity.
10 In robbery be not vaine,truft not
 yee in oppreffion:
if fo be riches doe increafe
 fet not your heart *thereon*.
11 The mighty God hath fpoken once:
 once & a aine thi word
I have it heard that *a"* power
 belongs unto the Lord.

        12 Alfo

12 Alfo to thee benignity
   o Lord, doth *appertaine*:
for thou according to his work
   rendreſt each man againe.

      Pſalme 63

A pſalme of David, when he was in the
   wildernes of Iudah.

O GOD, thou art my God, early
   I will for thee inquire:
my ſoule thirſteth for thee, my fleſh
   for thee hath ſtrong deſire,
In land whereas no water is
   that thirſty is & dry.

2 To ſee, as I ſaw in thine houſe
   thy ſtrength & thy glory.

3 Becauſe thy loving kindenes doth
   abundantly excell
ev'n life it ſelfe: wherefore my lips
   forth ſhall thy prayſes tell.

4 Thus will I bleſſing give to thee
   whilſt that alive am I:
and in thy name I will lift up
   theſe hands of mine on high.

5 My ſoule as with marrow & fat
   ſhall ſatiſſied bee:
my mouth alſo with joyfull lips
   ſhall prayſe give unto thee.

6 When as that I remembrance have
   of thee my bed upon,
and on thee in the night watches
   have meditation.

      O 2   7 Be.

7 Becaufe that thou haft been to me
   he that to me help brings;
therefore will I fing joyfully
   in fhaddow of thy wings.
8 My foule out of an ardent love
   doth follow after thee:
alfo thy right hand it is that
   which hath upholden mee.
9 But as for thofe that feek my foule
   to bring it to an end,
they fhall into the lower parts
   of the earth downe defcend.
10 By the hand of the fword alfo
   they fhall be made to fall:
and they be for a portion
   unto the Foxes fhall.
11 But the King fhall rejoyce in **God**,
   all that by him doe fweare
fhall glory, but ftopped fhall be
   their mouths that lyars are.

Pfalme 64
To the chief mufician, a pfalme
of David.

O GOD, when I my prayer make,
   my voyce *then* doe thou heare;
alfo doe thou preferve my life
   fafe from the enemies feare.
2 And from the fecret counfell of
   the wicked hide thou mee:
from th' infurection of them
   that work iniquitee.

                                                   who

3 Who have their tongue now sharpned
   like as it were a sword;
and bend *their bowes to shoot* their shafts
   ev'n a most bitter word:

4 That they in secrecie may shoot
   the perfect man to hitt.
suddenly doe they shoot at him,
   & never feare a whitt.

5 Them selves they in a matter ill
   encourage; how they may
lay snares in secret, thus they talk;
   who shall them see they say.

6 They doe search out iniquity,
   a search exact they keep:
both inward thought of euery man
   also the heart is deep.

7 But God shall shoot at them a shaft,
   be sudden their wound shall.

8 So that they shall make their owne tongue
   upon themselves to fall,
All that see them shall flee away.

9   All men shall feare, & tell
the works of God, for his doeing
   they shall consider well.

10 The just shall in the Lord be glad,
   and trust in him he shall:
and they that upright are in heart
   in him shall glory all.

Psalme 65

To the chief musician, a psalme and
song of David.

PSALM

O GOD, in Sion silently
   prayse wayteth upon thee:
and thankfully unto thee shall
   the vow performed bee.

2 O thou that harken dost unto
   the prayr that men doe make,
ev'n unto thee therefore all flesh
   themselves they shall betake.

3 Works of iniquitie they have
   prevailed against mee;
as for our trespasses they shall
   be purgde away by thee.

4 O blessed is the man of whom
   thou thy free choyee dost make;
and that he may dwell in thy courts
   him neere to thee dost take:
For with the good things of thy house
   be satisfyde shall wee;
and with the holy things likwise
   that in thy temple bee.

5 In righteousnes, thou, by the things
   that dreadfully are done,
wilt answer give to us, o God,
   of our salvation:
Vpon whom all the ends of th'earth
   do confidently stay,
& likwise they that are remov'd
   far off upon the sea.

6 He sets fast mountaines by his strength
7   girt with might. Hee doth swage
the noyse of seas, noyse of their waves

also

also the peoples rage.

(2)

8 They at thy tokens are afrayd
  that dwell in parts far out;
out goings of the morning thou
  and ev'ning makst to shout.

9 Thou visitest the earth,& dost
  it moisten plenteously,
thou with Gods streame,full of water
  enrichest it greatly:
When thou hast so prepared it,
  thou dost them corne prepare.

10 The ridces thou abundantly
  watrest that in it are;
The furrows of it thou setlest,
  with showers that do fall
thou makst it sofr;thou dost therof
  the springing blesse withall.

11 Thou dost the yeare with thy goodnes
  adorne as with a crowne,
also the paths where thou doit tread,
  fatnes they doe drop downe.

12 They drop upon the pastures that
  are in the wildernes;
and girded are the little hills
  about with joyfullnes.

13 Clothed the pastures are with flocks,
  corne over-covering
the valleys is;so that for joy
  they shout, they also sing.

P

PSALM lxvi.

To the chief muſician a pſalme or ſong.

O All yee lands, a joyfull noyſe
　　unto God doe yee rayſe.
2 Sing forth the honour of his name:
　　make glorious his prayſe.
3 How dreadfull in thy works art thou?
　　unto the Lord ſay yee:
　through thy powres greatnes thy foes ſhall
　　ſubmit themſelves to thee.
4 All they ſhall bow themſelves to thee
　　that dwell upon the earth,
　and ſing unto thee; they ſhall ſing
　　unto thy name with mirth.　　Selah.
5 Come hither, alſo, of the works
　　of God take yee notice,
　he in his doing terrible
　　towards mens children is.
6 He did the ſea into dry land
　　convert, a way they had
　on foot to paſſe the river through,
　　there we in him were glad.
7 He ruleth by his powre for ever,
　　his eyes the nations ſpie:
　let not thoſe that rebellious are
　　lift up themſelves on high.　　Selah.
8 Yee people bleſſe our God, & make　(2 part)
　　his prayſes voyce be heard.
9 Which holds our ſoule in life, our feet
　　nor ſuffers to be ſtird.
10 For God thou haſt us prov'd, thou haſt

us tryde as silver's tryde.

11 Into the net brought us,thou haſt
    on our loynes ſtreightnes tyde.

12 Men o're our heads thou madſt to ride,
    through fire & water paſſe
did wee,but us thou broughſt into
    a place that wealthy was.

13 With offrings I'le go to thine houſe:
    my vowes i'le pay to thee.

14 Which my lips uttred, & mouth ſpake,
    when trouble was on mee.

15 Burnt offrings I'le offer to thee
    that full of fatnes are,
with the incenſe of rams,I will
    bullocks with goates prepare.   *Selah.*

16 Come harken unto me all yee *(3 part)*
    of God that fearers are,
and what he hath done for my ſoule
    to you I will declare.

17 With mouth I cryde to him, & with
    my tongue extoll'd was hee.

18 If in my heart I ſin regard
    the Lord will not heare mee.

19 But God that is moſt mighty hath
    me heard aſſuredly;
unto the voyce of my prayr he
    liſt'ned-attentively.

20 Bleſt be the mighty God,becauſe
    neither my prayr hath hee,
nor yet his owne benignity,
    turned away from mee.

              P 2   PSALM

Pſalme 67

To the chief muſician on Negino.h
a pſalme or Song.

GOD gracious be to us,& give
his bleſſing us unto,
let him upon us make to ſhine
his countenance alſo.   Selah.

2 That there may be the knowledg of
thy way the earth upon,
and alſo of thy ſaving health
in every nation.

3 O God let thee the people prayſe,
let all people prayſe thee.

4 O let the nations rejoyce,
and let them joyfull bee:
For thou ſhalt give judgement unto
the people righteouſly,
alſo the nations upon earth
thou ſhalt them lead ſafely.   Selah.

5 O God let thee the people prayſe
let all people prayſe thee.

6 Her fruitfull increaſe by the earth
ſhall then forth yeilded bee:
God ev'n our owne God ſhall us bleſſe.

7 God I ſay bleſſe us ſhall,
and of the earth the utmoſt coaſts
they ſhall him reverence all.

Pſalme 68

To the chief muſician, a pſalme or ſong
of David.

pſalme

L Et God arise, his enemies
   let them dispersed bee,
  let them also that doe him hate
   away from his face flee.
2 As smoake is driven away, ev'n so
   doe thou them drive away:
  as wax at fire melts, in Gods sight
   let wicked so decay.
3 But let the righteous ones be glad:
   o let them joyfull bee
  before the Lord, also let them
   rejoyce exceedinglie.
4 Sing to God, to his name sing prayse,
   extoll him that doth ride
  on skies, by his name IAH; before
   his face joyfull abide.
5 A father of the fatherlesse,
   and of the widdows case
  God is a judge, & that within
   his holy dwelling place.
6 God seates the desolate in house,
   brings forth those that are bound
  in chaines, but the rebellious
   dwell in a barren ground.

(2)

7 O God when as thou didst goe forth
   in presence of thy folk,
  when through the desart wildernes
   thou diddest marching walk.   Selah.
8 The earth did at Gods presence shake,
   from heav'ns the drops downe fell:

P 3   Sinai

    the God of Ifraell.

9 O God thou on thy heritage
    didft fend a plenteous raine,
 whereby when as it weary was
    thou it confirm'd againe.

10 Thy congregation hath dwelt
    therin,thou doft prepare
 o God of thy goodnes,for them
    that poore afflicted are.

11 The Lord the word gave,great their troup
    that it have publifhed.

12 Kings of hoafts fled, fled, fhe that ftayd
    at home fpoyle devided.

13 Though yee have lyen among the pots,
    be like doves wings fhall yee
 with filver deckt, & her feathers
    like yellow gold that bee.

14 When there th'Almighty fcattred Kings,
    t'was white as Salmons fnow.

15 Gods hill like Bafhan hill, high hill,
    like Bafhan hill unto.

16 Why doe ye leap ye lofty hills?
    this is the very hill
 in which God loves to dwell, the Lord
    dwell in it ever will.

       (s)
17 Gods charrets twice ten thoufand fold,
    thoufands of Angells bee;
 with them as in his holy place,
    on Sinai mount is hee.

18 Thou didft afcend on high,thou ledft
    captivity caprive,   for

for men, yea, for rebells alſo   P S A- lx viii.
thou diddeſt gifts receive;
That the Lord God might dwell with them.

19   Who dayly doth us load
with benefits, bleſt be the Lord
that's our ſalvations God.   Selah.

20   He is God of ſalvation
that is our God moſt ſtrong:
and unto Iehovah the Lord
iſſues from death belong.

21   But God ſhall wound the enemies head,
the harry ſcalp alſo
of him that in his treſpaſſes
on forward ſtill doth go.

(4)

22   The Lord ſayd I'le bring back againe,
againe from Baſhan hill:
my people from the depths of ſeas
bring back againe I will.

23   That thy foot may be dipt within
blood of thine enemyes;
imbrude the tongue of thy dogs may
be in the ſame likewyſe.

24   They have thy goings ſeene o God
thy goings in progreſſe;
ev'n of my God my King within
place of his holyneſſe.

25   Singers went firſt, muſicians then,
in midſt maids with Timbrel.

26   Bleſſe God i'th Churches, the Lord from
the ſpring of Iſraell.

27   There litle Benjamin the chief
with Iudahs Lords,& their   counſel

counsell,with Zebulons princes,
    and Naphtalies lords were.
28 That valliant strength the which thou haft
    thy God hath commanded;
ftrengthen o God,the thing which thou
    for us haft effected.

(4)

29 For thy houfe at Ierufalem
    Kings fhall bring gifts to thee.
30 Rebuke the troups of fpearmen, troups
    of bulls that mighty bee:
  With peoples calves,with him that ftoops
    with pecces of filvar:
  o fcatter thou the people that
    delight themfelves in war.
31 Princes fhall out of Egipt come,
    & Ethiopias land
  fhall fpeedily unto the Lord
    reach her out-ftreched hand.
32 Earths kingdomes fing yee unto God:
    unto the Lord fing prayfe.   Selah.
33 To him that rides on heav'ns of heav'ns
    that were of ancient dayes:
  Loe,he his voyce, a ftrong voyce gives.
34   To God afcribe yee might,
 his excellence o're Ifraell is,
    & his ftrength in the height.
35 God fearfull from his holy place
    the God of Ifraell,hee
 gives ftrength & powre unto his folk,
    o let God bleffed bee.

psalme

PSALME lx ix.

To the chief muſician upon Shoſhannim,
A pſalme of David.

THe waters in unto my ſoule
   are come, o God,me ſave.
2 I am in muddy deep ſunk downe,
   where I no ſtanding have:
Into deep waters I am come,
   where floods mee overflow.
3 I of my crying weary am,
   my throat is dryed ſo;
Mine eyes faile: Iwayt for my God.
4   They that have hated mee
without a cauſe, then mine heads haires
   they more in number bee:
Alſo mine enemies wrongfully
   they are that would me ſlay,
mighty they are; then I reſtor'd
   what I took not away.
5 O God thou knowſt my fooliſhnes;
   my ſin's not hid from thee.
6 Who wayt on thee, Lord God of hoaſts,
   let not be ſhamd for mee:
O never ſuffer them,who doe
   for thee inquiry make,
o God of Iſraell, to be
   confounded for my ſake,

(2)

7 By reaſon that I for thy ſake,
   reproach have ſuffered:
confuſion my countenance
   hath overcovered.
      Q   8 I as

8 I as a stranger am become
   unto my bretherren,
and am an aliant unto
   my mothers childerren.
9 For of thy house the zeale me hath
   up eaten: every one
who thee reproach, their reproaches
   are fallen mee upon
10 In fasts, I wept & spent my soule,
    this was reproach to mee.
11 And I my garment sackcloth made:
    yet must their proverb bee.
12 They that do sit within the gate,
    against mee speak they do;
unto the drinkers of strong drink,
    I was a song also.
13 But I in an accepted time
    to thee Lord, make my prayr:
mee Lord, in thy salvations truth,
    in thy great mercy heare.

(3)

14 Deliver me out of the mire,
    and mee from sinking keep:
let mee be freed mine haters from,
    and out of waters deep.
15 O'reflow mee let not water floods,
    nor mee let swallow up
the deep, also let not the pitt
    her mouth upon mee shut.
16 Iehovah heare thou mee, for good
    is thy benignity:

turne

turne unto mee according to
greatnes of thy mercy.

17 And hide not thou thy countenance
from thy servant away;
because that I in trouble am;
heare me without delay.

18 O draw thou nigh unto my soule,
doe thou it vindicate;
give mee deliverance, because
of them that doe mee hate.

19 Thou haſt knowne my reproach, alſo
my ſhame, & my diſgrace:
mine adverſaryes every one
they are before thy face.

(4)

20 Reproach mine heart brake, I was griev'd:
for ſome me to bemone
I ſought, but none there was; & for
comforters, but found none.

21 Moreover in ſtead of my meate
unto mee gall they gave;
and in me thirſt they vineger
for drink made me to have.

22 Their table ſet before their face,
to them become a ſnare:
and *that let be* a trap, *which ſhould
have been* for *their* welfare.

23 And let their eyes be darkened,
that they may never ſee:
with trembling alſo make their loyres
to ſhake continuallie.

Q2   24 Poure.

24 Poure out thine ire on them, let seize
   on them thine anger fell,
25 Their Pallace let be desolate:
   none in their tents let dwell.
25 Because they *him* doe persecute
   on whom thy stroke is found:
   also they talk unto the grief
   of them whom thou dost wound.
27 Thou unto their iniquity
   iniquity doe add:
   into thy righteousnes for them
   let entrance none be had.
28 Out of the book of the living
   o doe thou them forth blor,
   and amongst them that righteous are
   be written let them not.
   (5)
29 But Lord, I'me poore & sorrowfull:
   let thy health lift me by.
30 With song I'le prayse the name of God:
   with thanks him magnify.
31 Vnto Iehovah *this* also
   shall be more pleasing far,
   then *any* oxe *or* bullock young,
   that horn'd & hoofed are.
32 This thing when as they shall behold,
   then shall be glad the meek;
   also their heart shall ever live
   that after God doe seek.
33 For the Lord hears the poore, nor doth
   despise whom he hath bound.

34 Let

34 Let heav'n, earth, seas & all therin
 that moves, his prayses sound.
35 For God will Iudahs cittyes build,
 and Sion he will save:
that they may dwell therin, & may
 it in possession have.
36 The seed also of his servants
 inherit shall the same:
also therin inhabit shall
 they that doe love his name.

Psalme 70

To the chief musician, a psalme to bring
 to remembrance.

O GOD, to rescue mee,
 Lord, to mine help, make hast.
2 Let them that after my soule seek
 asham'd be, & abasht:
Turnd back & shamd let them
 that in my hurt delight.
3 Turnd back let them ha, ha, that say,
 their shame for to requite.
4 Let all those that thee seek
 joy, & be glad in thee:
let such as lo e thy health say still,
 magnifyde let God bee.
5 Make hast to me Lord, for
 I poore am & needy:
thou art mine ayd, & my helper
 o Lord, doe not tarry.

Psalme 71

Q 3   PSALM

PSALM lxxi.

IEHOVAH, I for safety doe
betake my selfe to thee:
o let me not at any time
put to confusion bee.

2 Me rescue in thy righteousnes,
let me deliverance have:
to me doe thou incline thine eare,
also doe thou me save.

3 Be thou my dwelling Rock, whereto
I alwayes may resort:
thou gav'st commandment me to save,
for thou my Rock & Fort.

4 Out of the hand of the wicked
my God, deliver mee,
out of the hand of the unjust,
leaven'd with crueltie.

5 For thou o God, Iehovah art
mine expectation:
and thou art hee whom from my youth
my trust is set upon :

6 Thou hast upheld mee from the womb,
thou art he that tookst mee
out of my mothers belly; still
my prayse shall be of thee.

(2)

7 To many I a wonder am
but thou my refuge strong.
8 Let my mouth fill'd be with thy prayse,
& honour all day long .
9 Within the time of elder age
o cast me not away,

and

and doe not thou abandon me
    when my strength doth decay.
10 Because they that be enemyes
    to me, against me spake,
and they that for my soule lay-wayt,
    counsell together take.
11 Saying, God hath forgotten him:
    doe yee him now pursue,
and apprehend him, for *there is*
    not one him to rescue.
12 Depart not farre from mee, o God,
    my God hast to helpe mee.
13 The adversaryes of my soule,
    let them ashamed bee:
Let them consumed be, let them
    be also covered,
both with reproach & dishonour,
    that for my hurt wayted.

(3)
14 But *I* with patience will wayt
    on thee continuallee,
and *I* will adde yet more & more
    to all the prayse of thee.
15 My mouth forth shall thy righteousnes,
    and thy salvation show
from day to day, for *of the same*
    no number doe I know.
16 In the strong might of God the Lord
    goe on a long will *I*:
I'le mention make of thy justice,
    yea ev'n of thine only.

17 from

17 From my youth up o mighty God,
    thou halt inftructed mee:
  and hitherto I have declar'd
    the wonders wrought by thee.
18 And now unto mine elder age,
    and hoary head, o God,
  doe not forfake mee: till I have
    thy power fhowne abroad,
  Vnto this generation,
    and unto every one
  that fhall hereafter be to come,
    thy ftrong dominion.

(4)

19 Thy righteoufnes o God, it doth
    reach up on high alfo,
  great are the things which thou haft done;
    Lord who's like thee unto?
20 Thou who haft caufed mee to fee
    afflictions great & fore,
  fhalt mee revive, & me againe
    from depths of earth reftore.
21 Thou fhalt my greatnes multiply
    & comfort me alwayes.
22 Alfo with tuned *Pfaltery*
    I will fhew forth thy prayfe,
  O thou my God, I will fing forth
    to thee mine Harp upon,
  thy verity & faithfullnes,
    o Ifraels Holy-one.
23 My lips with fhouting fhall rejoyce
    when I fhall fing to thee:

my

my foule alfo, which freely thou
  haft brought to liberty.
24 Likewife my tongue fhall utter forth
  thy juftice all day long:
for they confounded are, & brought
  to fhame, that feek my wrong.

Pfalme 72

A pfalme for Solomon.

O GOD, thy judgements give the King,
  & thy juftice to the Kings Sonne.
2 He fhall thy folk with juftice judge,
  & to thy poore fee judgement done,
3   The mountaines fhall abundantly
unto the people bring forth peace:
the little hills fhall bring the fame,
by executing righteoufnes.
4   Poore of the people he fhall judge,
and children of the needy fave;
& he in peeces fhall break downe
each one that them oppreffed have.
5   They fhall thee feare, while Sun & moon
endure through generations all.
6 Like raine on mowne graffe he fhall come:
as fhowres on earth diftilling-fall.
7   The juft fhall flourifh in his dayes,
& ftore of peace till no moone bee.
8 And from the fea unto the fea,
from floud to lands end reigne fhall hee.
9   They that within the wildernes
doe dwell, before him bow they muft:
and they who are his enemies

K

they

they verily shall lick the dust.

(2)

10 Vpon him presents shall bestow
of Tarshish, & the Iles, the Kings,
Shebahs, & Sebahs Kings also,
shall unto him give offerings.

11 Yea to him all the kings shall fall,
& serve him every nation:

12 For needy crying save he shall,
the poore, & helper that hath none.

13 The poore & needy he shall spare,
and the soules of the needy save.

14 Their soules from fraud & violence
by him shall free redemption have:
And pretious in his sight shall be

15 the bloud of them. And he shall live,
and unto him shall *every one*
of purest gold of Shebah give:
Also each one their humble prayr
in his behalfe shall make alwayes:
and every one his blessednes
shall dayly celebrate with prayse.

(3)

16 Of corne an handfull there shall be
ith land the mountains tops upon,
the fruit whereof shall moving shake
like to the trees of Lebanon:
And they that of the citty be
like grasse on earth shall flourish all.

17 His name for ever shall indure
as long as Sun continue shall:

So shall his name continued be,
and men in him themselves shall blesse,
and all the nations of the world
shall him the blessed.one professe.

18 O let Iehovah blessed be,
the God, the God of Israell,
hee worketh by himselfe alone
such things whereat men may marvell.

19 And blessed be his glorious name.
for ever, let the whole earth be
fill'd full with glory of the same,
Amen, also Amen *say wee.*

This.   After the common tunes.

19 And aye be blest his glorious name,
also let the earth all
be filled with his glorious fame,
Amen, & so it shall.

---

20   The prayers of David, the
Son of Iesse, are
ended.

THE

THIRD BOOKE.

Psalme 73
A psalme of Asaph.

TRuly to Israell God is good,
 to men of a cleane heart.
2 But my feet almost slipt, my steps
 aside did well nigh start.
3 For I was envious at the fooles,
 in peace to see the ill.
4 For in their death no bands there are,
 but firme their strength is still.
5 Like other meane men they are not
 in toylesome misery,
nor are they stricken with like plagues
 as other mortals bee.
6 Therefore doth pride like to a chaine
 encompesse them about,
and like a garment, violence
 doth cover them throughout.
7 Within the fatnes *which they have*
 extended are their eyes:
greater prosperity they have
 then their hearts can devise.
8 Corrupt they are, & wickedly
 speak guile: proudly they talk.
9 Against the heav'ns they set their mouth,
 their tongue through th'earth doth walk.

       to There

(2)

10 Therefore his people unto them
  have hither turned in,
and waters out of a full cup
  wrung out to them have been.
11 And they have sayd, how can it be
  that God this thing should know,
& is there in the highest one
  knowledge hereof also?
12 Loe, these are the ungodly ones
  who have tranquillity:
within the world they doe increase
  in rich ability.
13 Surely in vaine in purity
  cleansed my heart have I.
14 And hands in innocence have washt,
  for plagu'd am I dayly:
And every morning chastened.
15   If I think thus to say,
  thy childrens generation
    loe then I should betray;
16 And when this poynt to understand
  casting I did devis:,
the matter too laborious
  appeared in mine eyes.
17 Vntill unto the sanctuary
  of God I went, & then
I prudently did understand
  the last end of these men.
  (4)
18 Surely in places slippery

R 3   these

these men thou placed hast:
and into desolations
   thou dost them downward cast.
19 As in a moment, how are they
   brought to destruction?
how are they utterly consum'd
   with sad confusion?
20 Like to a dreame when as a man
   awaking doth arise,
so thou o God, when thou awakst
   their Image shalt despise.
21 My heart thus was leaven'd with grief,
   prickt were my reins by mee:
22 So foolish was I, & knew not,
   like a beast before thee.

(4)

23 Neverthelesse continually
   before thee I doe stand:
thou hast upheld mee stedfastly
   also by my right hand.
24 Thou with thy prudent counsell shalt
   guidance unto mee give:
up afterward also thou shalt
   to glory mee receive.
25 In heavn above but thee alone
   who is it that I have?
and there is nothing upon earth
   besides thee that I crave.
26 This flesh of mine, my heart also
   doth faile me altogether:
but God the strength is of my heart,

            and

and portion mine for ever.

27 For loe, they that are far from thee
 utterly perish shall:
those who a whoring goe from thee
 thou hast destroyed all.

28 But as for mee, for mee it's good
 neere God for to repaire:
in God the Lord I put my trust,
 all thy works to declare.

Psalme 74

Maschil of Asaph.

O GOD, why hast thou cast us off,
 why doth thy rage indure?
for ever smoaking out against
 the sheep of thy pasture?

2 Thy congregation call to minde
 of old by thee purchast:
the rod of thine inheritance
 which thou redeemed hast,
This mount Sion wherin thou dwelst.

3 Lift up thy foot on hye,
unto the desolations
 of perpetuity:
Thy foe within the Sanctuary
 hath done all lewd designes.

4 Amidst thy Church thy foes doe roare:
 their Banners set for signes.

5 The man that axes on thick trees
 did lift up had renowne:

6 But now with axe & maules at once,
 her carv'd works they beat downe.

7 Thy

7 Thy sanctuaryes into fire
　　they cast, the dwelling place
　of thy name downe unto the ground
　　prophanely they did raze.

8 Let us together them destroy,
　　thus in their hearts they sayd:
　Gods Synagogues throughout the land
　　all in the flames they layd.

(?)

9 Our signes we see not, there's no more
　　a Prophet us among:
　nor with us any to be found
　　that understands how long.

10 How long shall the oppressing foe
　　o mighty God, defame?
　thine enemy for evermore
　　shall he blaspheme thy name?

11 Why dost thou thus withdraw thine hand,
　　the right hand of thy strength?
　out of thy bosom o doe thou
　　draw it forth to the length.

12 Because the mighty God hath been
　　from ancient time my King,
　in middest of the earth he is
　　salvation working.

13 Thou diddest by thy mighty powre
　　devide the sea asunder:
　the Dragons heads in peeces thou
　　didst break the waters under.

14 The heads of the Leviathan
　　thou into peeces brake:.

to

to people that in defarts dwell
for meat thou didft him make.

15 Thou clav'ft the fountain & the floud,
thou dri'dft up flouds of might.

16 Thine is the day, & night is thine:
thou Sun prepar'ft, & light.

17 Thou all the borders of the earth
haft conftituted faft :
the fummer & the winter cold
the fame thou formed haft

(:)

18 Remember this, the enemy
reproachfully doth blame,
o Lord, alfo the foolifh folk
blafphemed have thy name.

19 O doe not to the multitude
thy turtles foule deliver:
the congregation of thy poore
forget not thou for ever.

20 Vnto thy cov'nant have refpect:
becaufe the dark places
of th'earth with habitations
are full of furioufnes.

21 O let not the oppreffed one
returne away with fhame:
o let the poor & needy one
give prayfe unto thy name.

22 Arife o God, plead thine owne caufe:
have thou in memorie
how day by day the foolifh man
with fcorne reproacheth thee.

S   Thre

23 Thine enemyes voyce forget not thou:
the loud tumult of those
continually on high ascends
that rise thee to oppose.

Psalme 75

To the chief musician Altaschith, psalme
or song of Asaph.

O GOD, to thee doe we give thanks,
thanks give we unto thee:
& that thy name is neere at hand,
thy wonders shew to bee.

2 When I th'assembly shall receive
uprightly judge I will.

2 Th'earth & its dwellers all do melt:
I stay its pillars still,

4 I did unto the foolish say,
deale not so foolishly:
also unto the wicked ones,
lift not the horne on hye.

5 Lift yee not up your horne on high:
with stiffned neck speak not,

6 For neither from East, West, nor South,
promotion can be got.

7 But God is judge: he sets up one,
another downe doth tread.

8 For in the Lords hand is a cup,
also the wine is red:
It's full of mixture, & thereout
he poures: but on earth all
the wicked ones the dregs therof
both strein, & drink them shall.

9 But as for me I will declare,

for

for evermore I will
sing prayses unto him that is
the God of Iacob *still.*

10 Of men ungodly all the hornes
also cut off will I:
but the hornes of the righteous,
shall be exalted high,

Psalme 76

To the chief musician, on Neginoth, a psalm
or song of Asaph.

IN Iudah God is knowne: his name
is great in Israell.

2 In Salem also is his tent:
in Sion he doth dwell,

3 There brake he th'arrows of the bow,
the shield, sword, & battell.   Selah.

4 Illustrious thou art, thou dost
the mounts of prey excell.

5 They that are stout of heart are spoyld,
they slept their sleep profound:
and of the men of might there is
none that their hands have found.

6 Of Iacob o thou mighty God.
as thy rebuke out past,
the chariot also, & the horse
in a dead sleepe are cast.

(2)

7 Thou ev'n thou art to be feared
and who is it before
thy presence that can stand, when as
that thou art angry sore?

8 Thou diddest cause for to be heard

judgement from heav'n above:
the earth exceedingly did feare,
   also it did not move.
9 When as the mighty God arose,
   to th' execution
of judgement, to save all the meek
   that are the earth upon.   Selah.
10 Assuredly unto thy prayse,
   shall turne the wrath of man:
& the remainder of the earth
   also thou shalt restraine.
11 Vow, & pay to the Lord your God;
   that him surround all yee,
and bring ye presents unto him,
   that feared ought to bee.
12 The spirit that in Princes is,
   asunder cut he shall:
unto the Kings on earth that be,
   dreadfull he is *withall*.

Psalme 77

To the chief musician, to Ieduthun, a
psalme of Asaph.

TO GOD I cryed with my voyce:
   yea with my voyce I have
cryed unto the mighty God;
   and eare to mee he gave.
2 In my distresse I sought the Lord;
   my sore ran in the night,
& ceased not: also my soule
   refused comfort quite.
3 I did remember God, also

disqu

disquieted was I:
I did complaine, & my spirit
o'rewhelmd was heavily.   Selah.
4 Awaking thou dost hold mine eyes:
I cannot speak for feares.
5 I have considered dayes of old,
of ancient times the yeares.

(2)

6 To my remembrance I doe call
the song in night I had:
I commun'd with my heart, also
strict search my spirit made.
7 For ever will the Lord cast off?
& pleasd will he not bee?
8 His tender mercy is it ceast
to perpetuitee:
His promise doth it, faile for aye?
9 Hath God forgot likewise
gracious to be? hath he shut up
in wrath his deare mercyes?   Selah.
10 Then did I say, within my selfe,
tis mine infirmity:
the yeares of the right hand I will
think on of the most high.

(3)

11 I will unto remembrance call
the actions of the Lord:
thy wondrous works of ancient time
surely I will record.
12 I'le muse also of all thy works,
& of thy doings talk.

S. 3   13 with.

13 Within the temple is thy way,
o God, *where thou doſt walk.*
What god ſo great as our God is?

14 Works wonderfull that are
thou God haſt done; among the folk
thou doſt thy ſtrength declare.

15 Thoſe that thy people are thou haſt
with thine owne armé ſet free,
of Iacob alſo of Ioſeph
the childeren that bee.   Selah.

(4)

16 Thee did the waters ſee, o God,
thee did the waters ſee:
they were afraid, the deeps alſo
could not but troubled bee.

17 With waters were the clouds pour'd forth,
the ſkies a ſound out ſent:
alſo thine arrows on each ſide
abroad diſperſed went.

18 Thy thunders voyce in heaven was:
the world illuminate
thy lightnings did, the earth alſo
trembled & ſhook hereat.

19 Thy wayes ith ſea, thy paths & ſteps
unkowne, are in the deep.

20 By Moſes & by Arons hand
thou ledſt thy folk like ſheep.

Pſalme 78
Maſchil of Aſaph.

Give liſtning eare unto my law,
yee people that are mine,

unto

142

unto the sayings of my mouth
    doe yee your eare incline.
2 My mouth I'le ope in parables,
    I'le speak hid things of old:
3 Which wee have heard & knowne:& which
    our fathers have us told.
4 Them from their children wee'l not hide,
    to th'after age shewing
the Lords prayses: his strength, & works
    of his wondrous doing.
5 In Iacob he a witnesse set,
    & put in Israell
a law, which he our fathers charg'd,
    they should their children tell:
6 That th'age to come & children which
    are to be borne might know;
that they might rise up & the same
    unto their children show.
7 That they upon the mighty God
    their confidence might set:
and Gods works & his commandment
    might keep & not forget,
8 And might not like their fathers be,
    a stiffe, stout race; a race
that set not right their hearts: nor firme
    with God their spirit was.
        (2)
9 The armed sonnes of Ephraim,
    that went out with their bowe,
did turne their backs in the day when
    they did to battell goe.

                    10 Gods

10 Gods cov'nant they kept not: to walk
    in his law they denyde:
11 His works, & wonders, they forgot,
    that he to them defcryde.
12 Things that were mervielous he did
    within their fathers fight:
    in Egipts land, within the field
    of Zoan, *by his might.*
13 He did devide the fea, alfo
    he cauf'd them through to paffe:
    & he the waters made to ftand
    that as an heap it was.
14 With cloud by day, with fire all night
15   he led them; Rocks he clave
    in wildernes, as from great deeps
    drink unto them he gave.
16 Ev'n from out of the ftony rock
    ftreames he did bring alfo,
    & caufed water to run downe
    like as the rivers do.
(3)
17 Moreover they did adde yet more
    againft him for to fin:
    by their provoaking the moft high
    the wildernes within.
18 And alfo they within their heart
    did tempt the God of might:
    by afking earneftly for meat
    for their foules appetite:
19 Moreover they againft God fpake:
    they fayd can God be able

within

within the defart wildernes
　　to furnifh us a table?
20 Loe, he the rock fmote, thence gufht out
　　waters, & ftreames did flow:
for his folk can he flefh provide,
　　can he give bread alfo?
21 The Lord heard, he was wroth for this,
　　fo kindled was a fire
'gainft Iacob:&'gainft Ifraell
　　there came up wrathfull ire.
22 For they in God believed not:
　　nor in his health did hope:
23 Though from above he charg'd the clouds:
　　& doores of heav'n fet ope:
(4)
24 Manna to eate he raind on them;
　　& gave them the heavns wheat.
25 Each man of them ate Angells food:
　　to th'full he fent them meate.
26 Ith heav'ns he made the Eaft-winde blow:
　　brought South-winde by his powre.
27 He flefh on them like duft: wing'd foules
　　like the feas fand did fhowre.
28 And in the middeft of their camp
　　he caufed it to fall,
ev'n round about on every fide
　　their dwelling places all.
29 So they did eate, they filled were
　　abundantly alfo:
for that which was their owne defire
　　he did on them beftow:
　　　　　　　　T　　　　　　30 How-

145

30 Howbeit they were not eſtrang'd
   from their luſtfull deſire:
  but while their meat was in their mouths,
31 Vpon them came Gods ire,
   And ſlew their fat ones: & ſmote downe
   of Iſraell the choiſe men.
32 Still for all this they ſin'd: nor did
   believe his wonders then.

(5)

33 Therefore he did in vanity
   the dayes of their life ſpend,
  and haſtily he brought their yeares
   vnto a fearfull end.
34 When he them ſlew, then after him
   they ſought with their deſire:
  and they return'd, early alſo
   did after God enquire.
35 Likewiſe that God was their ſtrong rock
   they cal'd to memoree:
  and that the mighty God moſt high,
   was their Redeemer free.
36 Yet with their mouth they flattred him:
   and to him their tongues lyde.
37 For right their heart was not in them:
   nor did in's cov'nant byde.
38 But full of mercy, he forgave
   their ſin, & ſtroyd them not;
  yea, oft he turn'd his wrath aſide,
   nor rayſ'd all's anger hot.
39 For he, that they were but fraile fleſh,
   and as it were a winde

that

that paſſeth, & comes not againe,
recalled unto minde.

(6)

40 How oft in deſart vext they him:
and made him there to moane?

41 Yea, they turn'd, tempted God: & did
ſtint Iſr'ells holy one.

42 His hand they did not, nor the day
keep in their remembrance:
wherein he from the enemy
gave them deliverance:

43 And how his ſignes miraculous
in Egipt he had ſhowne:
and his moſt fearfull prodigies
within the field of Zoan:

44 Alſo how he their rivers had
converted into bloud:
& (that they could not drink therof)
the waters of their floud.

45 Amongſt them, which did them devoure,
he ſent forth divers flies:
& them amongſt, which them deſtroyd,
he ſent forth frogs likewiſe.

46 He gave their fruit to th'Caterpillar:
their labour to th'Locuſt.

47 He did their Vines deſtroy with haile:
their Sycamores with froſt.

48 Alſo unto the haile he did
their cattell ſhut up faſt:
likewiſe their heards of cattell to
the fiery thunder blaſt

T 2   49 He

49 He cast on them fierce ire, & wrath,
    & indignation,
  & sore distresse: by sending forth
    ill Angells them upon.

(7)

50 He made a way unto his wrath,
    and their soule did not save
from death: also their life over
    to Pestilence he gave,
51 He within Egipt land also
    all the first borne did smite:
those that within the tents of Ham,
    were chiefest of their might:
52 But he made like a flock of sheep
    his owne folk forth to go:
like to a flock ith wildernes
    he guided them also.
53 And he in safety did them lead
    so that they did not dread:
within the sea their enemies
    he also covered.
54 And to the border he did bring
    them of his holy place:
unto this mountaine which he did
    by his right hand purchase.
55 Fore them he cast the heathen out,
    their lot he did devide
by line: & Isr'ells tribes he made
    in their tents to abide.

(8)

56 Yet they tempted the most high God,

                and

& griev'd him bitterly:
also his teftimonyes they
kept not *attentively*:

57 But like their fathers back they turn'd
and faithlefneffe did fhow:
they turned were afide ev'n like
to a deceitfull bowe.

58 For they to anger did provoake
him with their places hye:
& with their graven Images,
mov'd him to jealoufy.

59 God hearing this, was wroth, & loath'd
Ifr'ell with hatred great:

60 So Shiloh s tent he left: the tent
which men among ft he fet,

61 And he delivered his ftrength
into captivity:
alfo into the enemies hand
his beautifull glory.

62 To th' fword he gave his folk: & was
wroth with his heritage.

63 Fire their young men devour'd:their maides
none gave to marriage.

64 Their Priefts fell by the fword: alfo
their widdows did not weepe.

65 Then did the Lord arife as one
awakned out of fleepe:
Like a ftrong man that after wine

66 doth fhout. He alfo fmote
his foes behinde: & fo he gave
them an eternall blot.

T 3   67 Then

(9)

67 Then he did Iosephs tent refufe:
nor Ephr'ims tribe approv'd.
68 But he the tribe of Iudah chofe:
mount Sion which he lov'd.
69 And he his Sanctuary built
like unto places high:
like to the earth which he did found
to perpetuity.
70 Of David alfo his fervant.
election he did make,
and from the place of folding up
the fheep he did him take.
71 From following the ewes with young
he did him then advance;
to feed Iacob his folk, alfo
Ifr'ell his heritance.
72 So he according to his hearts
integrity them fed:
and by the wife difcretion
of his hands he them led.

Pfalme 79
A pfalme of Afaph.

O GOD, the heathen entred have
thine heritance, & defylde
thine holy temple: they on heaps
Ierufalem have pylde.
2 The dead bodyes of thy fervants
they given have for meate
to th' fowles of heav'n: flefh of thy Saints
for beafts of earth to eate.

2 Their

3 Their bloud they have forth powred round
    about Ierusalem
  like unto waters: & there *was*
    none for to bury *them*.

4 To those that neere unto us dwell
    reproach become are wee:
  a scoffing & a scorne to them
    that round about us bee.

5 How long, Iehovah, wilt thou still
    continue in thine ire,
  for ever? shall thy jealousie
    burne like as doth the fire?

6 Vpon the heathen poure thy wrath
    which never did thee know,
  upon the kingdomes that have not
    cal'd on thy name also.

7 Because they Iacob have devour'd:
    his habitation
  they also wondrously have brought
    to desolation.

(:)

8 Minde not against us former sins,
    let thy mercies make hast
  us to prevent: because we are
    neere utterly layd waste.

9 God of our safety, help thou us
    for thy names glory make,
  us free also, & purge away
    our sin for thy names sake.

10 Why say the heathen where's their God
    with heathen let be knowne

                              before

before our eyes, the vengeance of
   thy servants bloud out flowne.
11 Before thee let the prisoners sighs
   come up, accordingly
as is thy mighty arme: save those
   that are design'd to dye,
12 And to our neighbours seven fold,
   into their bosome pay,
that their reproach, with which o Lord,
   reproached thee have they.
13 So we thy folk & pasture sheepe,
   will give thee thanks alwayes:
and unto generations all,
   wee will shew forth thy prayse.

Psalme 80

To the chief musician upon Shoshannim
Eduth, a psalme of Asaph.

O Isr'ells shepheard, give thou eare;
   that Ioseph leadst about
like as a flock: that dwelst betweene
   the Cherubims, shine out.
2 Before Ephr'im & Benjamin,
   Manasseh s tribe also,
doe thou stir up thy strength, & come,
   and to us safety show.
3 O God returne thou us againe,
   and cause thy countenance
to shine forth upon us; so wee
   shall have deliverance.
4 Lord God of hoasts, how long wilt thou
   be wroth at thy folks prayrs?

thou

PSALME lxxx.

5 Thou feedst with bread of tears, & them
  to drink giv'st many teares.
6 A strife unto our neighbours us
  thou dost also expose:
  and scornefully amongst themselves
  laugh at us doe our foes.
7 O God of hoasts, turne us againe,
  & cause thy countenance
  to shine forth upon us, so wee
  shall have deliverance.

(2)

8 Thou hast brought out of Egipt land
  a Vine, thou diddest cast
  the heathen people forth, also
  this *vine* thou planted hast.
9 Before it thou prepared hast
  a roome where it might stands
  deep root thou didst cause it to take
  and it did fill the land.
10 Her shade hid hills, & her boughs did
  like Cedars great *extend*.
11 Her boughs to th'sea, & her branches
  she to the floud did send.
12 Why hast thou then her hedges made
  quite broken downe to lye,
  so that all those doe pluck at her
  that in the way passe by?
13 The Boare from out the wood he doth
  by wasting it annoy:
  & wilde beasts of the field doe it
  devouringly destroy.

14 Wee

(s)

14 Wee doe beseech thee to returne
    o God of hoasts, incline
  to look from heaven, & behould,
    & visit thou this vine.

15 The vineyard which thou hast also
    with thy right hand set fast,
  that branch likewise which for thy selfe
    strongly confirm'd thou hast.

16 It is consumed with the fire
    and utterly cut downe,
  perish they doe, & that becuase
    thy countenance doth frowne.

17 Vpon the man of thy right hand
    let thine hand present bee:
  upon the son of man whom thou
    hast made so strong for thee.

18 So then from henceforth wee will not
    from thee goe back at all:
  o doe thou quicken us, & wee
    upon thy name will call.

19 Lord God of hoasts, turne us againe,
    and cause thy countenance
  to shine forth upon us, so wee
    shall have deliverance.

Psalme 81

To the chiefe musician upon Gi'tith,
a psalme of Asaph.

S Ing unto God who is our strength,
    and that with a loud voyce:
  unto him that is Iacobs God

make

make yee a joyfull noyſe.

2 Take up a pſalme of melodie,
   and bring the Timbrel hither:
the Harp *which ſoundes* ſo pleaſantly
   with Pſaltery together.

3 As in the time of the new moone
   with Trumpet ſound on high:
in the appoynted time & day
   of our ſolemnity.

4 Becauſe that unto Iſraell
   this thing a ſtatute was;
and by the God of Iacob this
   did for a judgement paſs.

5 This witneſſe he in Ioſeph ſet
   when as through Egipt land
he went: I there a language heard
   I did not underſtand.

6 I from the burden which he bare
   his ſhoulder did ſet free:
his hands alſo were from the pots
   delivered by mee.

(2)

7 Thou cal'dſt in ſtreights, & I thee freed:
   in thunders ſecret way
I anſwred thee, I prov'd thee at
   waters of Meribah.   Selah.

8 Heare o my peop'e, & I will
   teſtifie unto thee:
o Iſraell, if that thou wilt
   attention give to mee.

9 Any ſtrange god there ſhall not be

V 2

in

in midft of thee at all:
nor unto any forrein god
   thou bowing downe fhalt fall.
10 I am the Lord thy God who thee
from land of Egipt led:
   thy mouth ope wide, & thou by mee
   with plenty fhalt be fed.
11 My people yet would not give eare
unto the voyce I fpake:
   and Ifraell would not in mee
   quiet contentment take.
12 So in the hardnes of their heart
I did them fend away,
in their owne confultations
   likewife *then* walked they.

(3)

13 O that my people unto mee
obedient had bin:
and o that Ifraell he had
   walked my wayes within.
14 I fhould within a little time
have pulled downe their foes:
I fhould have turn'd my hand upon
   fuch as did them oppofe.
15 The haters of the Lord to him
obedience fhould have faynd:
but unto perpetuity
   their time fhould have remaind.
And with the fineft of the wheat
have nourifht them fhould hee:
with honie of the rock I fhould

have

have satisfied thee.

Psalme 82

A psalme of Asaph.

THe mighty God doth stand within
   th'assemblie of the strong:
and he it is that righteously
   doth judge the gods among.

2 How long a time is it that yee
   will judge unrighteouslie?
   & will accept the countenance
   of those that wicked bee?

3 See that yee doe defend the poore,
   also the fatherlesse:
unto the needy justice doe,
   and that are in distresse.

4 The wasted poore, & those that are
   needy deliver yee;
and them redeeme out of the hand
   of such as wicked bee.

5 They know not, nor will understand
   in darknes they walk on:
all the foundations of the earth
   quite out of course are gone.

6 I sayd that yee are gods, & sonnes
   of th'highest yee are all.

7 But yee shall dye like men, & like
   one of the princes fall.

8 That thou mayst judge the earth o God,
   doe thou thy selfe advance;
for thou shalt have the nations
   for thine inheritance.

V 3   PSALM

PSALM lxxxiii.

Pſalme 83

A pſalme or ſong of Aſaph,

O GOD, doe not thou ſilence keep:
o doe not thou refraine
thy ſelfe from ſpeaking, & o God.
doe not thou dumb remaine.

2 For loe, thine enemies that be
doe rage tumultuouſly:
& they that haters be of thee
have lift the head on hye.

3 Againſt thoſe that thy people be
they crafty counſell take;
alſo againſt thy hidden ones
they conſultation make.

4 They ſayd, leſt they a nation be,
let's cut them downe therefore,
that in remembrance Iſr'ells name
may not be any more.

5 For they together taken have
counſell with one conſent,
and in confederation
againſt thee they are bent.

6 The tabernacles of Edom
and of the Iſhmaelites:
the people of the Haggarens
& of the Moabites.

7 The men of Gebal, with Ammon,
and Amaleck conſpire,
the Philiſtims, with them that be
inhabitants of Tyre.

8 Aſſyria morover is

con-

conjoyned unto them:
& help they have adminiftred
unto Lots childerren.

(2)

9 As thou didft to the Middianites,
so to them be it dor e:
as unto Sifera & Iabin
at the Brook of Kifon

10 Who neere to Endor fuddenly
were quite difcomfited:
who alfo did become as dung
that on the earth is *fpred.*

11 Like unto Oreb, & like Zeeb
make thou their Nobles fall,
yea, as Zeba & Zalmunna
make thou their Princes all.

12 Who fayd, for our poffeffion
Gods houfes let us take.

13 My God, thou like a wheel, like ftraw
before the winde them make.

14 As fire doth burr e a wood, & as
the flame fets hills on fire:

15 So with thy tempeft them purfue,
& fright them in thine ire.

16 Doe thou their faces all fill full
of ignominious fhame:
that fo they may o Lord, be made
to feek after thy name.

17 Confounded let them ever be,
and terrible troubled:
yea, let them be put unto fhame,

and

PSALM lxxx iii, lxxx iv.

and bee extinguished.

18 That men may know; that thou whose name
IEHOVAH is only,
art over all the earth throughout
advanced the most high.

Psalme 84

To the chief musician upon *Gittith* a psalm
for the sonnes of *Korah*.

HOw amiable Lord of hoasts
thy tabernacles bee?
2 My soule longs for Iehovahs courts,
yea it ev'n faints in mee.
Mine heart, my flesh also cryes out
after the living God:
3 Yea ev'n the sparrow hath found out
an house *for hir aboad*.
Also the swallow *findes* her nest
thine Altars *neere unto*
where shee her young layes: Lord of hoasts,
my King, my God also.
4 Blest they that dwell within thy house:
still they will give thee prayse.   Selah.
5 Blest is the man whose strength's in thee,
in whose heart are their wayes.
6 Who as they passe through Baca's Vale
doe make it a fountaine:
also the pooles *that arether in*
are filled full of raine:
7 From strength to strength they go: to God
in Sion all appeare.
8 Lord God of hoasts, o heare my pra'yr,
o Iacobs

o Iacobs God, give eare.   Selah.

(2)

9 Behould o God our shield: the face
  of thine annoynted see.

10 For better's in thy courts a day,
   then *elswhere* thousands bee:
   I rather had a doore-keeper
     be it'h house of my God:
   then in the tents of wickednes
     to settle mine aboad.

11 Because the Lord God is a Sun,
     he is a shield also:
   Iehovah *on his people* grace
     and glory will bestow:
   No good thing will he hould from them
     that doe walk uprightlee.

12 O Lord of hoasts, the man is blest
     that purs his trust in thee.

Psalme 85

To the chiefe musician, a psalme for the
sonnes of Korah.

O LORD, thou hast been to the land
  gracious: Iacobs captiuity
  thou hast returned *with thy hand.*

2 Thou *also* the iniquity
    of thy people hast pardoned:
    thou all their sin hast covered.   Selah.

3 Thou all thine anger didst withdraw:
    from thy fierce indignation
    thou hast thy selfe turned away.

4 O God of our salvation

                    W   convert

Convert thou us; & doe thou make
thine anger toward us to flake.

5 Shall thy wrath ever be us on?
wilt thou thine indignation
draw out to generation?
and unto generation?

6 Wilt thou not us reviv'd let bee,
that thy folk may rejoyce in thee.

(2)

7 Lord on us shew thy mercy, eke
thy saving health on us bestow.

8 I'le hark what God the Lord will speak,
for hee'l speak peace his folk unto,
and to his Saints: but let not them
to foolishnes returne agen.

9 Surelyhis saving health is nigh
unto all them that doe him feare;
that in our land may dwell glory.

10 Mercy & truth met *together*,
prosperity & righteousnes
embracing did *each other* kiss.

11 Truth springs out of the earth: also
from heaven looketh righteousnes.

12 Yea, God shall that that's good bestow.
our land eke shall give her increase.

13 Iustice shall goe before his face,
& in the way her steps shall place.

Another of the same

O LORD, thou favour'd hast thy land:
Jacobs captivity.

2 Thou hast brought back: thou pard'ned hast
thy

thy folks iniquity:
Thou haft clofe coverd all their fin.
3   Thy wrath away all caft
thou haft: from fiercenes of thine ire
thy felfe return'd thou haft.
4   Convert us back, o thou the God
of our falvation:
& toward us caufe thou to ceafe
thine indignation,
5 Wilt thou be angry ftill with us
for evermore? what fhall?
thine anger be by thee drawne-out
to generations all?
6 Wilt thou not us revive? in thee
thy folk rejoyce fhall fo.
7 Shew us thy mercy, Lord; on us
thy faving health beftow.

(2)

8 I'le heare what God the Lord will fpeak;
for to his people peace
hee'l fpeak; & to his Saints: left they
returne to foolifhnes.
9 Surely naere them that doe him feare
is his falvation:
that glory may within our land
have habitation.
10 Mercy & truth doe joyntly meet:
juftice & peace doe kiffe.
11 Truth fprings from earth: & rightoufnes
from heaven looking is.
12 Yea what is good the Lord fhall give:

W 2   and

and yeild her fruit our land.

11 Iuſtice ſhall 'fore him goe: & make
her ſteps i'th way to ſtand.

Pſalme 86
A prayer of David.

BOw downe o Lord, thine eare,
& harken unto mee:
becauſe that I afflicted am,
alſo I am needie.

2 Doe thou preſerve my ſoule,
for gracious am I:
o thou my God, thy ſervant ſave,
that doth on thee rely.

3 Lord pitty me, for I
cry daily thee unto.

4 Rejoyce thy ſervants ſoule: for Lord.
to thee mine lift I do.

5 For thou o Lord, art good,
to pardon prone withall:
and to them all in mercy rich
that doe upon thee call.

6 Iehovah, o doe thou
give eare my pray'r unto:
& of my ſupplications
attend the voyce alſo.

7 In day of my diſtreſſe,
to thee I will complaine:
by reaſon that thou unto mee
wilt anſwer give againe.

(2)

8 Amongſt the gods, o Lord,

164

none is there like to thee:
neither with thine are any works
   that may compared bee.
9   All nations o Lord,
   whom thou haſt made, *the ſame*
ſhall come & worſhip thee before:
   and glorify thy Name.
10   Becauſe thou mighty art,
   the things that thou haſt done
are wonderfull, thou art thy ſelfe
   the mighty God alone.
11   Iehovah, unto mee
   o make thy way appeare,
walk in thy truth I will; mine heart
   unite thy name to feare.
12   Withall mine heart I will
   o Lord my God, thee prayſe:
& I will glorify thy name,
   for evermore *alwayes.*
13   Becauſe that unto mee
   thy mercy doth excell;
alſo thou haſt delivered
   my ſoule from loweſt hell.
       (3)
14   O God, the proud, & troups
   of violent roſe 'gainſt mee,
after my ſoule they ſought: nor have
   before them placed thee.
15   But Lord thou art a God,
   tender, & gracious;
longſuffring, & in mercy thou
        W 3   and

& truth art plenteous.

16   O turne thou unto mee,
      and mercy on mee have:
  unto thy servant give thy strength:
     thine handmaides son do save.

17   Mee shew a signe for good,
      that mine haters may see,
 and be asham'd; because Lord, thou
    dost help, & comfort mee.

Psalme 87

A psalme or song for the sonnes
of Korah.

A Mong the holy hills
   is his foundation.

2 More then all Iacobs tents, the Lord
    loves the gates of Sion.

3   Things glorious spoken are
     o Gods citty, of thee.   Selah.

4 I'le mention Rahab, & Babel,
    to them that doe know mee;
    Behold Philistia,
    Tyrus *citty* likewise,
with Ethiopia; that this man
    by birth did thence arise.

5   Also it shall be sayd,
    of Sion that borne there
this & that man was, & the high'st
    himselfe shall stablish her.

6   Iehovah he shall count,
    ev'n at that time when as,
the people he doth number up,

that

that there this man borne was.   Selah

7   Both those that singers are
      as also *there shall bee,*
    those that on instruments doe play;
      all my springs are in thee.

Psalme 88

A song or psalme for the sons of Korah, to
the chief musician upō Mahalath Leannoth,
        Maschil of Heman the
          Ezrahite.

LORD God of my salvation,
    before thee day & night cryde I.
2   Before thee o let my pray'r come:
    incline thine eare unto my cry.
3   Because my soule is troubled so:
    and my life draws nigh to the grave.
4   Counted with them to'th pit that go:
    I'me as a man that no strength have.
5   Free among those men that be dead,
    like slaine which in the grave are shut;
    by thee noe more remembered:
    and by thy hand off are they cut.
6   Thou hast mee layd i'th pit most low
    in darknesses, within deep caves.
7   Hard on mee lyes thy wrath, & thou
    dost mee afflict with all thy waves.   Selah·
8   Men that of mine acquaintance bee
    thou hast put far away mee fro:
    unto them loathsome thou madst mee,
    I am shut up nor forth can go.
9   Because of mine affliction,

                              mine

mine eye with mourning pines away:
Iehovah, I call thee upon:
& ftretch my hands to thee all day;

(2)

10   Shew wonders to the dead wilt thou?
fhall dead arife & thee confefs?   Selah.

11   I'th grave wilt thou thy kindenes fhow?
in loft eftate thy faithfullnes?

12   Thy works that wonderfull have been
within the dark fhall they be knowne?
& fhall thy righteoufnes *be feene*
in the land of oblivion?

13   But Lord I have cryde thee unto
at morne, my pray'r prevent fhall thee.

14   Lord why cafts thou my foule thee fro?
why hideft thou thy face from mee?

15   I'me poore afflicted, & to dye
am ready, from my youthfull yeares,
I am fore troubled doubtfully
while I doe beare thy horrid feares.

16   Thy fierce wrath over mee doth goe,
thy terrors they doe mee difmay.

17   Encompaffe mee about they doe,
clofe mee together all the day.

18   Lover & friend a far thou haft
removed off away from mee,
& mine acquaintance thou haft caft
into dark fom obfcuritee.

Pfalme 69
Mafchil of Ethan the
Ezrahite.

PSALM

PSALME lxxxix.

THe mercyes of Iehovah sing
　　for evermore will I:
I'le with my mouth thy truth make known
　　to all posterity.

2 For I have sayd that mercy shall
　　for ever be up built;
establish in the very heav'ns
　　thy faithfullnes thou wilt.

3 With him that is my chosen one
　　I made a covenant:
& by *an oath* have sworne unto
　　David mine owne servant.

4 To perpetuity thy seed
　　establish-sure I will:
also to generations all
　　thy throne I'le build up *still*.　　Selah.

5 Also the heav'ns thy wonders Lord,
　　they shall with prayse confess;
in the assemblie of the Saints
　　also thy faithfullnes.

6 For who can be compar'd unto
　　the Lord the heav'ns within?
'mong sonnes of mighty to the Lord
　　who is't that's like to him.

(2)

7 I'th Saints assemblie greatly God
　　is to be had in feare:
and to be reverenc't of all those
　　that round about him are.

8 Lord God of hoasts, what Lord like thee
　　in power doth abide?

X

thy

thy faithfullnes doth compasse thee
  also on every side.
9 Over the raging of the sea,
  thou doft dominion beare:
when as the waves therof arise,
  by thee they stilled are.
10 Like to one slaine, thou broken haft
  in pieces Rahab quite:
thou haft disperst thine enemies
  ev'n by thine arme of might.
11 The heav'ns together with the earth,
  thine are they: thine they bee;
the world, with fullnes of the same,
  founded they were by thee.
12 The North together with the South
  thou didft create the same:
Tabor together with Hermon,
  rejoyce shall in thy Name.
(3)
13 Thou haft a very mighty arme,
  thy hand it is mighty,
and also thy right hand it is
  exalted up on high.
14 Iuftice & judgement of thy throne
  are the prepared place:
mercy & truth preventing shall
  goe forth before thy face.
15 O blessed are the people that
  the joyfull found doe know,
Lord, in thy countenances light
  they up & downe shall goe:

                 16 They

16 They shall in thy name all the day
    rejoyce exceedingly:
and in thy righteousnes they shall
    be lifted up on high.

17 Because that thou art unto them
    the glory of their powre:
our horne shall be exalted high,
    also in thy favour.

18 Because Iehovah is to us
    a safe protection;
and he that is our Soveraigne,
    is Isr'ells Holy one.

(4)

19 Then didst thou speake in vision,
    unto thy Saint, & sayd,
I upon one that mighty is
    salvation have layd:
One from the folk chose, I set up.

20 David my servant I
have found: him I annoynted with
    mine oyle of sanctity.

21 With whom my hand shall stablisht be;
    mine arme him strengthen shall.

22 Also the enemy shall not
    exact on him at all:
Nor shall the Son of wickednes
    afflict him any more.

23 Before him I'le beat downe his foes,
    and plague his haters sore.

24 My mercy, truth, shall be with him;
    & in my name shall be

X 2

his

25 his horne exalted. And I'le set
    his hand upon the sea:
I'th rivers also his right hand.

26   He shall cry mee unto,
    thou art my Father: & my God,
    Rock of my health also.

27 Also I will make him to be
    my first begotten one:
higher then those that Princes are,
    who dwell the earth upon.

28 My mercy I will keep for him
    to times which ever last:
also my covenant with him
    it shall stand very fast.

(5)

29 And I will make his seed indure
    to perpetuitee:
his throne likewise it like unto
    the dayes of heav'n shall bee.

30 If that his sons forsake my law,
    & from my judgements swerve:

31 If they my stattutes break, & my
    commandes doe not observe:

32 Then will I visit with the rod
    their bold transgression,
as also their iniquity
    with sore stripes *them upon*.

33 But yet my loving kindenes, is
    I'le not take utterly
away from him: nor will suffer
    my faithfullnes to lye.

34 The

34 The covenant I made with him
  by mee shall not be broke:
neither will I alter the thing
  which by my lips is spoke.
35 Once sware I by my holines,
  if I to David lye:
36 His seed asuredly shall last
  to perpetuity:
And like the Sun 'fore mee his throne.
37   It like the moone for aye
shall be establish't, like a true
  witnesse in heav'n: Selah.

(6)

38 But thou hast cast off, & us had
  in detestation:
exceedingly thou hast been wroth
  with thine annoynted one.
39 Thou hast made voyd the covenant
  of thy servant, his crowne
thou hast prophan'd unto the ground
  by casting of it downe.
40 Thou hast broke all his hedges downe:
  his forts thou ruin'd hast.
41 All those doe make a spoyle of him
  who by the way have past:
Hee's a reproach to his neighbours.
42   Of them that him annoy
thou hast advanced their right hand:
  & made all's foes to joy.
43 The sharp edge also of his sword
  thou hast turn'd backward quite:

X 3   and

and in the battell thou haſt not
   made him to ſtand upright.
44 Thou haſt made alſo for to ceaſe
   his glorious renowne:
unto the very earth his throne
   thou alſo haſt caſt downe.
45 And of his youthfull yeares the dayes
   thou haſt diminiſhed;
with very great confuſion
   thou haſt him covered.   Selah.

(7)
46 How long? Iehovah, wilt thou hide
   thy ſelfe for evermore?
burne like unto confuming fire
   ſhall thy diſpleaſure ſore?
47 To thy remembrance doe thou call
   how ſhort a time have I;
wherefore haſt thou created all
   mens ſonnes to vanity?
48 What ſtrong man is there that doth live,
   & death ſhall never ſee?
from the ſtrong power of the grave
   ſhall he his ſoule ſet free?
49 Thy former loving kindeneſſes
   o Lord, where are they now?
which in thy truth & faithfullnes
   to David thou didſt vow.
50 Lord, the reproach of thy ſervants
   unto remembrance call:
how I itbeare in my boſome
   from mighty people all.

51 Wher-

51 Wherewith thy adverfaryes Lord,
    have caſt reproach upon,
  wherewith they have reproacht the ſteps
    of thine annointed one.
52 O let Iehovah be bleſſed
    to all eternitee:
  Amen, *ſo let it be*, alſo
    Amen, *ſo it ſhall bee.*

THE

FOVRTH BOOKE

Pſalme 90.

A prayer of Moſes the man of God.

O LORD, thou haſt been unto us
    from generation,
to generation, a place
  of fixed manſion.
2 Before the mountaines were brought forth,
    ere earth & world by thee
were form'd: thou art eternally
  God to eternitee.
3 Thou doſt unto deſtruction
    turne miſerable men:
and then thou ſayſt yee ſonnes of men
  doe yee returne agen.
4 For why o Lord, a thouſand yeares
    are but within thy ſight
as yeſterday when it is paſt

                      and

and as a watch by night.
5 By thee like as it were a flood
  they quite away are borne,
 they like a sleep, & as the grasse
  that grows up in the morne.
6 It in the morning flourisheth,
  it also up doth grow;
 it in the ev'ning is cut downe
  it withereth also.
7 Because wee by thine anger are
  consumed speedily:
 and by thy sore displeasure wee
  are troubled suddenly.
8 Thou hast set our iniquityes
  before thee in thy sight:
 our secret evills are within
  thy countenances light.
9 Because in thine exceeding wrath
  our dayes all passe away:
 our years wee have consumed quite,
  ev'n as a tale *are they.*
(2)
10 Threescore & ten yeares are the dayes
  of our yeares which remaine,
 & if through strength they fourscore be,
  their strength is grief & paine:
 For it's cut off soone, & wee flye
11 away: Who is't doth know
 thine angers strength? according as
  thy feare, thy wrath is so.
12 Teach us to count our dayes: our hearts

so

So wee'l on wisdome set.

13 Turne Lord, how long? of thy servants
    let it repent thee yet?
14 O give us satisfaction
    betimes with thy mercee:
that so rejoyce, & be right glad,
    through all our dayes may wee.
15 According to the dayes *wherin*
    affliction wee have had,
and yeares *wherin* wee have seen ill,
    now also make us glad.
16 Vnto those that thy servants be
    doe thou thy work declare:
also thy comely glory to
    those that thy children are.
17 Let our Gods beauty be on us,
    our handy works also
stablish on us; our handy work
    establish it doe thou.

Psalme 91.

HE that within the secret place
    of the most high doth dwell,
he under the Almightyes shade
    shall lodge himselfe *full well.*
2 My hope he is, & my fortresse,
    I to the Lord will say:
he is my God, & I in him
    my confidence will stay.
3 Surely out of the fowlers snare
    he shall deliver thee,
also thee from the Pestilence

        Y   *infect.*

infectious shall free.

4 He with his feathers hide thee shall,
    under his wings shall bee
thy trust: his truth shall be a shield
    and buckler unto thee.

5 Thou shalt not be dismaide with feare
    for terrour by the night:
nor for the arrow that with speed
    flyeth in the day light:

6 Nor for the Pestilence that doth
    walk in the darknes fast:
nor for the sore destruction
    that doth at noone day wast.

(2)

7 A thousand shall fall at thy side,
    & ten thousand also
at thy right hand, but it shall not
    approach thee neere unto:

8 Only thou with thine eyes this thing
    attentively shalt view:
also thou shalt behold how that
    the wicked have their due.

9 Because Iehovah who hath been
    my safe protection,
ev'n the most high, thou hast him made
    thine habitation.

10 Not any thing that evill is
    there shall to thee befall,
neither shall any plague come nigh
    thy dwelling place at all.

11 Because that he his Angells will

               comand

command concerning thee:
in all thy wayes *where thou doſt* walk
   thy keeper for to bee.
12 They ſhall ſupport thee in their hands:
   leſt thou againſt a ſtone
13 ſhouldſt daſh thy foot. Thou trample ſhalt
   on th'Adder, & Lion:
The Lion young & Dragon thou
   ſhalt tread under thy feet.
14 I will deliver him, for hee
   on mee his love hath ſet:
Becauſe that he hath knowne my Name,
   I will him ſet on high.
15 Vpon mee he ſhall call in pray'r,
   and anſwer him will I:
I will be with him when he is
   in troubleſome diſtreſſe,
& I to him will honour give,
   when I ſhall him releaſe.
16 With dayes of long continuance
   I'le give to him his fill:
& alſo my ſalvation
   declare to him I will.

Pſalme 92.

A pſalme or ſong for the
Sabbath day.

IT is a good thing to give thanks
   Iehovah thee unto:
unto thy Name prayſes to ſing,
   o thou moſt high alſo.
2 Thy loving kindenes to ſhew forth
       Y 2   with

within the morning light:
also thy truth, & faithfullnes,
to shew forth every night.

3 Vpon a ten string'd instrument,
and Psaltery upon:
upon the solemne sounding Harp,
a meditation.

4 For through thy work, o Lord, thou hast
mee caused to rejoyce:
and in the workings of thy hands
I will triumph with voyce.

5 O Lord, how mighty are thy works:
thy thoughts are very deepe.

6 The bruitish knows nor; nor the foole
this in his heart doth keepe.

7 When as the wicked doe spring up
ev'n like the grasse unto,
& all that work iniquity
when as they flourish do:
It's that they then may be destroy'd
to perpetuity.

8 But thou Iehovah dost abide
for evermore most high.

9 For loe, thy foes, for loe, o Lord,
thy foes they perish shall:
the workers of iniquity
they shall be scattred all.

(2)

10 But like the Vnicornes my horne
thou shalt exalt on high:
& with fresh oyle in mine old age

annoynted

annoynted be shall I.

11 Also mine eye shall see my wish
upon mine enemyes:
mine eare shall heare of wicked ones,
that up against me rise.

12 Like to the Palme tree flourish shall
he that is righteous:
like to a Ceadar he shall grow
that is in Lebanus.

13 They that within Iehovahs house
are planted *stedfastly*:
within the Courts of our God they
shall flourish *pleasantly*.

14 Their fruit they shall in their old age
continue forth to bring:
they shall be fat, yea likewise they
shall still be flourishing:

15 To shew that upright is the Lord:
my refuge strong is hee,
also that there is not in him
any iniquitee.

Psalme 9t.

THe Lord reigns, cloth'd with majesty:
God cloath'd with strength, doth gird
himselfe· the world so stablisht is,
that it cannot be stir'd.

2 Thy throne is stablished of old:
3 from aye thou art. Their voyce
the flouds lift up, Lord, flouds lift up,
the flouds lift up their noyse.

4 The Lord on high then waters noyse

Y 3

more

more strong then waves of sea:
5 Thy words most sure: Lord, holines
    becomes thine house for aye.

Psalme 94

O LORD God, unto whom there doe
    revenges appertaine:
  o God, to whom vengeance belongs,
    clearly shine forth againe.

2 Exalt thy selfe, o thou that art
    Iudge of the earth throughout:
  render a recompence unto
    all those that are so stout.

3 Iehovah, o how long shall they
    that doe walk wickedly?
  how long shall those that wicked are
    rejoyce triumphingly?

4 How long shall those men utter forth
    & speake things that hard bee?
  & shall all such thus boast themselves.
    that work iniquitee?

5 Lord, they thy folk in pieces break:
    & heritage oppress.

6 They slay the widdow, & stranger,
    & kill the fatherless.

7 The Lord they say, yet shall not see:
    nor Iacobs God it minde.

8 Learne vulgar Sots: also yee fooles
    when will yee wisdome finde?

9 Who plants the eare, shall he not heare?
    who formes the eye, not see?

10 Who heathen smites, shall he not check?

mans

mans teacher, knows not hee?

(2)

11 The Lord doth know the thoughts of man,
    that they are very vaine.
12 Bleſt man whom thou correctſt, o Lord;
    & in thy law doſt traine.
13 That thou mayſt give him quiet from
    dayes of adverſity:
  untill the pit be digged for
    ſuch as doe wickedly.
14 Becauſe Iehovah he will not
    his people caſt away,
  neither will hee forſake his owne
    inheritance for aye.
15 But judgement unto righteouſnes
    it ſhall returne agen:
  alſo all upright ones in heart
    they ſhall purſue it *then.*
15 Againſt the evill doers, who
    will up for mee ariſe?
  who will ſtand up for mee 'gainſt them
    that work iniquityes?
17 Had not the Lord me helpt: my ſoule
    had neere in ſilence dwel'd.
18 When as I ſayd, my foot ſlips: Lord,
    thy mercy mee upheld.

(3)

19 Amidſt the multitude of thoughts
    of mine within my minde,
  ſtill from thy conſolations
    my ſoule delight doth finde.

20 Shall

20 Shall the throne of iniquity
     have fellowship with thee:
which frameth molestation
     and that by a decree?
21 They joyntly gathered themselves,
     together they withstood
the soule of him that righteous is:
     & condemne guiltlesse blood.
22 But yet Iehovah unto mee
     he is a refuge high:
also my God he is the rock
     of my hopefull safety.
23 Their mischief on them he shall bring,
     & in their wickednes
he shall them cut off : yea, the Lord
     our God shall them supprefs.

          Psalme 95.

O Come, let us unto the Lord
     shout loud with singing voyce,
to the rock of our saving health
     let us make joyfull noyse.
2 Before his presence let us then
     approach with thanksgiving:
also let us triumphantly
     with Psalmes unto him sing.
3 For the Lord a great God: & great
     King above all gods is.
4 In whose hands are deepes of the earth,
     & strength of hills are his
5 The sea to him doth appertaine,
     also he made the same:

                              and

& also the drye land is his
 for it his hands did frame.
6 O come, & let us worship give.
 & bowing downe adore:
he that our maker is, the Lord
 o let us kneele before.
7 Becauſe he is our God, & wee
 his paſture people are,
 & of his hands the ſheep: to day
 if yee his voyce will heare,
8 As in the provocation,
 o harden not your heart:
as in day of temptation,
 within the vaſt deſart.
9 Whē mee your fathers tryde, & pro'vd,
 & my works lookt upon:
10 Fourty yeares long I griev'd was with
 this generation:
And ſayd, this people erre in heart:
 my wayes they doe not know.
11 To whom I ſware in wrath: if they
 into my reſt ſhould goe.

Pſalme 96.

Sing to the Lord a new ſong: ſing
 all th'earth the Lord unto:
2 Sing to Iehovah, bleſſe his Name,
 ſtill his ſalvation ſhow.
3 To'th heathen his glory, to all
 people his wonders ſpread.
4 For great's the Lord, much to be prayſ'd,
 above all gods in dread.

Z

Becauſe

PSALM xCvi.

5 Becaufe vaine Idols are they all
    which heathens Gods doe name:
but yet Iehovah he it is
    that did the heavens frame.

6 Honour & comely majefty
    abide before his face:
both forritude & beauty are
    within his holy place.

7 Yee kindreds of the people *all*
    unto the Lord afford,
glory & mightynes alfo
    give yee unto the Lord.

8 The glory due unto his name
    give yee the Lord unto;
offer yee an oblation,
    enter his courts alfo.

(*c*)

9 In beauty of his holynes
    doe yee the Lord adore:
the univerfall earth *likewife*
    in feare ftand him before.

10 'Mong heathens fay, Iehovah reigns:
    the world inftablenes
fhall be, unmov'd alfo: he fhall
    judge folk in righteoufnes.

11 O let the heav'ns *therat* be glad,
    & let the earth rejoyce:
o let the fea, & it's fullnes
    with roaring make a noyfe.

12 O let the field be full of joye,
    & all things there about:

then

then all the trees that be i'th wood
they joyfully shall shout
13 Before Iehovah, for he comes,
he comes earths judge to bee.
the world with justice, & the folke
judge with his truth shall hee.

Psalme 97

THe Lord doth reigne, the earth
o let heerat rejoyce:
the many Isles with mirth
let them lift up their voyce.

2   About him round
dark clouds there went,
right & judgement
his throne doe found.

3   Before him fire doth goe,
& burnes his foes about.

4   The world was light also
by lightnings he sent out:
the earth it saw
& it trembled.

5   The hills melted
like wax away
At presence of the Lord:
at his presence who is
of all the earth the Lord.

6   That righteousnes of his
the heavens high
they doe forth show:
all folk also
see his glory.

Z 2

7 who

7. Who graven Images
doe ſerve, on them remaine
let dreadfull ſhamefullnes:
& who in Idols vaine
themſelves doe boaſt:
with worſhip bow
to him all you
Gods Angells *hoſt*.

8 Sion heard, & was glad,
glad Iudahs daughters were,
this cauſe, ō Lord, they had,
thy judgements did appeare.

9 For Lord thou high
all earth ſet o're:
all Gods before
in dignity.

10 Yee that doe love the Lord,
the evill hate doe yee;
to his Saints ſoules afford
protection doth hee:
he will for them
freedome command
out of the hand
of wicked men.

11 For men that righteous are
ſurely there is ſowne light:
& gladnes for their ſhare
that are in heart upright.

12 Ioy in the Lord,
yee Iuſt confeſſe;
his holyneſſe

while

while yee record.
Pſalme 9 8.
A Pſalme

A New ſong ſing unto the Lord,
  for wonders he hath done:
his right hand & his holy arme
  him victory hath wonne.

2 Iehovah his ſalvation
    hath made for to be knowne:
  his righteouſnes i'th heathens ſight
    hee openly hath ſhowne.

3 To iſr'ells houſe of his mercy
    & truth hath mindefull been:
  the ends of all the earth they have
    our Gods ſalvation ſeene.

4 Vnto Iehovah all the earth,
    make yee a joyfull noyſe:
  make yee alſo a cheerfull ſound,
    ſing prayſe, likewiſe rejoyce.

5 With Harp ſing to the Lord; with Harp,
    alſo with a Pſalms voyce.

6 With Trumpets, Cornets ſound; before
    the Lord the King rejoyce.

7 The ſea let with her fullnes roare:
    the world, & there who dwell.

8 O let the flouds clap hands: let hills
    rejoyce together well

9 Before the Lord, for he doth come
    to judge the earth: rightly
  with juſtice ſhall he judge the world,
    & folk with equity.
              Z 3   PSALM

Pſalme 99.

IEHOVAH 'tis that reigns,
 let people be in dread:
  'midſt Cherubs he remaines,
  th'earth let itbe moved.

2 Iehovah is
 in Sion great,
 in highnes ſet
  he is likewiſe
 Above all the people.

3 Let them confeſſe thy Name
 ſo great & terrible:
 for holy is the ſame.

4 The King his might
 doth love juſtice:
 thou doſt ſtabliſh
  things that be right:
 Iudgement thou doſt, alſo
 in Iacob righteouſnes.

5 The Lord our God doe you
 ſet up in his highnes,
  & worſhip yee
 his footſtoole at:
 by reaſon that
  holy is hee.

6 Moſes alſo Aron
 among his Prieſts, likewiſe
 Samuell all thoſe among
 that to his name ſend cryes:
  called they have
 the Lord upon,

and

and he *alone*
   them anſwer gave.
7 He unto them did ſpeake
   it'h cloudy pillar: *then*
   they kept his records, eke
   his ord'nance he gave them.
8   Lord, thou who art
   our God didſt heare,
   & didſt anſwer
    to them impart,
   Thou waſt a God pard'ning
   them, although thou vengeance
   upon their works didſt bring.
9 The Lord our God advance,
   & bow yee downe
   at's holy hill:
   for our God's *ſtill*
   the Holy-one.

Pſalme 100.

A *Pſalme* of prayſe.

Make yee a joyfull ſounding noyſe
   unto Iehovah, all the earth:
2 Serve yee Iehovah with gladnes:
   before his preſence come with mirth.
3   Know, that Iehovah he is God,
   who hath us formed it is hee,
   & not our ſelves: his owne people
   & ſheepe of his paſture are wee.
4   Enter into his gates with prayſe,
   into his Courts with thankfullnes:
   make yee confeſſion unto him,

                        and

& his name reverently bleſſe.

5   Becauſe Iehovah he is good,
for evermore is his mercy:
& unto generations all
continue doth his verity.

Another of the ſame.

MAke yee a joyfull noyſe unto
   Iehovah all the earth:
2 Serve yee Iehovah with gladnes:
   before him come with mirth.
3 Know, that Iehovah he is God,
   not wee our ſelves; but hee
hath made us. his people, & ſheep
   of his paſture are weo.
4 O enter yee into his gates
   with prayſe, & thankfullneſſe
into his Courts: confeſſe to him,
   & his Name doe yee bleſſe.
5 Becauſe Iehovah he is good,
   his bounteous-mercy
is everlaſting: & his truth
   is to eternity.

Pſalme 101.

A pſalme of David.

MErcy & judgement I will ſing,
   Lord, I will ſing to thee.
2 I'le wiſely doe in perfect way:
   when wilt thou come to mee?
I will in midſt of my houſe walk
   in my hearts perfectnes:
3 I will not ſet before mine eyes

matter

matter of wickednes:
I hate their worke that turne aside,
it shall not cleave mee to.

4 Froward in heart from mee shall part,
none evill will I know.

5 I'le cut him off, that slaundereth
his neighbour privily:
I cannot beare the proud in heart,
nor him that looketh high.

6 Vpon the faithfull in the land
mine eyes shall be, that they
may dwell with mee: he shall mee serve
that walks in perfect way.

7 Hee that a worker is of guile,
shall not in my house dwell:
before mine eyes he shall not be
setled, that lies doth tell.

8 Yea, all the wicked of the land
early destroy will I:
to cutt off from Gods citty all
that work iniquity.

Psalme 102

A prayer of the afflicted when he is over-
whelmed, & poureth out his complaint
before the Lord.

LORD, heare my supplication,
& let my cry come thee unto:

2 I'th day when trouble is on mee,
thy face hide not away mee fro:
Thine eare to mee doe thou incline,
i'th day I cry, soone answer mee:

A a

3 For

PSALM CII.

3 For as the smoake my dayes consume,
& like an hearth my bones burnt bee.

4 My heart is smote, & dryde like grasse,
that I to eate my bread forget:

5 By reason of my groanings voyce
my bones unto my skin are set.

6 Like Pelican in wildernes,
like Owle in desart so am I:

7 I watch, & like a sparrow am
on house top solitarily.

8 Mine enemies daily mee reproach:
'gainst mee they rage, 'gainst mee they sweare:

9 That I doe ashes eate for bread:
& mixe my drink with weeping-teare.

10 By reason of thy fervent wrath
& of thy vehement-disdaine:
for thou hast high advanced mee,
& thou hast cast mee downe againe.

(2)

11 My dayes as shaddow that decline:
& like the withered grasse am I.

12 But thou, Lord, dost abide for aye:
& thy Name to eternity.

13 Thou wilt arise, & wilt shew forth
thy tender-mercy on Sion:
for it is time to favour her,
yea the set time is now come on.

14 For in her stones thy servants doe
take pleasure, & her dust pitty.

15 And heathens shall the Lords Name feare.
& all Kings of th'earth thy glory.

16 When

194

16   When as the Lord ſhall Sion build
hee in his glory ſhall appeare.

17 The poor's petition hee'l regard,
   & hee will not deſpiſe their pray'r.

18   This ſhall in writing be inroll'd
for the ſucceeding-after-race:
that people alſo which ſhall bee
created, they the Lord may prayſe.

19   For from his Sanctuary high
from heavn's the Lord the earth doth ſee

20 To heare the groanes of priſoners:
to looſe them that deaths children bee.

21   The Lords prayſe in Ieruſalem:
his Name in Sion to record.

22 when people are together met,
   & Kingdomes for to ſerve the Lord.

(3)

23   He weakned hath i'th way my ſtrength,
& ſhortened my dayes hath hee.

24 I ſayd, in middeſt of my dayes
my God doe not away take mee:
Thy yeares throughout all ages are.

25 Thou haſt the earth's foundation layd
for elder time: & heavens bee
the work which thine owne hands have made.

25   They periſh ſhall, but thou ſhalt ſtand:
they all as garments ſhall decay:
& as a wearing veſtiment
thou ſhalt the change, & chang'd are they.

27   But thou art ev'n the ſame: thy yeares
they never ſhall conſumed bee.

28 Thy

23 Thy servants children shall abide,
  & their seed stablisht before thee.
  Psalme 103.
  A psalme of David.

O Thou my soule, Iehovah blesse,
  & all things that in me
most inward are, in humblenes
  his Holy-Name blesse ye

2 The Lord blesse in humility,
  o thou my soule: also
put not out of thy memory
  all's bounties, thee unto.

3 For hee it is who pardoneth
  all thine iniquityes:
he it is also who healeth
  all thine infirmityes.

4 Who thy life from destruction
  redeems: who crowneth thee
with his tender compassion
  & kinde benignitee.

5 Who with good things abundantlee
  doth satisfie thy mouth:
so that like as the Eagles bee
  renewed is thy youth.

6 The Lord doth judgement & justice
  for all oppressed ones.

7 To Moses shew'd those wayes of his:
  his acts to Isr'ells sonnes.
  (2)

8 The Lord is mercifull also
  hee's very gracious:

and

and unto anger hee is flow,
  in mercy plenteous.
9 Contention he will not maintaine
  to perpetuity
nor he his anger will retaine
  unto eternity.
10 According to our fins *likewise*
  to us hee hath not done:
nor hath he our iniquityes
  rewarded us upon.
11 Becaufe even as the heavens are
  in height the earth above:
fo toward them that doe him feare
  confirmed is his love.
12 Like as the Eaft & *Weft* they are
  farre in their diftances:
he hath remov'd away fo far
  from us our trefpaffes.
13 A fathers pitty like unto,
  which he his fonnes doth beare:
like pitty doth Iehovah fhow
  ro them that doe him feare.
14 For he doth know this frame of ours:
  he minds that duft wee bee.
15 Mans dayes are like the graffe: like flowrs
  in field, fo flourifheth hee.
16 For over it the winde doth paffe,
  & it away doth goe;
alfo the place wheras it was
  noe longer fhall it know.

Aa3   17 But

(3)

17 But yet Gods mercy ever is,
    shall be,& aye hath been
  to them that feare him; and's justice
    unto childrens children.

18 To such as keepe his covenant,
    that doe in minde up lay
  the charge of his commandement
    that it they may obey.

19 The Lord hath in the heavens hye
    established his throne:
  and over all his Royallty
    doth beare dominion.

20 O yee his Angells that excell
    in strength, blesse yee the Lord
  that doe his word, that harken well
    unto the voyce of 's word.

21 All yee that are the Lords armies,
    o blesse Iehovah *still*:
  & all yee ministers of his,
    his pleasure that fullfill.

22 Yea, all his works in places all
    of his dominion,
  blesse yee Iehovah: o my Soul,
    Iehovah blesse *alone*.

Psalme 104.

THe Lord blesse,o my Soule, o Lord
    my God, exceedingly
  great art thou: thou with honour art
    cloath'd & with majesty.

2 Who dost thy selfe with light, as if

it

it were a garment cover:
who like unto a curtaine dost
    the heavens stretch all over.
4 Who of his chambers layes the beames
    ith waters, & hee makes
the cloudes his Charrets, & his way
    on wings of winde hee takes.
5 His Angells Spirits, his ministers
    who makes a fiery flame.
5 who earths foundations layd, that ne're
    should be remov'd the same.
6 Thou with the deep (as vith a robe)
    didst cover the *dry land*:
above the places mountainous
    the waters they did stand.
7 When as that thou rebukedst them
    away then fled they fast:
they also at thy thunders voyce
    with speed away doe hast.
8 Vp by the mountaines they ascend:
    downe by the valleys go,
the place which thou didst found for them
    untill they come unto.
9 Thou hast to them a bound prefixt
    which they may not passe over:
10 that they might noe more returne
    againe the earth to cover.

(2)

10 who springs into the valleys sends,
    which run among the hills.
11 whence all beasts of the field have drink:

                wilde

wilde asses drink their fills.

12 Heavns fowles dwell by them, which do sing
    among the sprigs with mirth.

13 Hee waters from his lofts the hills:
    thy works fruit fill the earth.

14 For beasts hee makes the grasse to grow,
    herbs also for mans good:
    that hee may bring out of the earth
    what may be for their food:

15 Wine also that mans heart may glad,
    & oyle their face to bright:
    and bread which to the heart of man
    may it supply with might.

16 Gods trees are sappy: his planted
    Cedars of Lebanon:

17 Where birds doe nest: as for the Storke,
    Firres are her mansion.

18 The wilde Goates refuge are the hills:
    rocks Conies doe inclose.

19 The Moone hee hath for seasons set,
    the Sun his setting knows.

(3)

20 Thou makest darknes, & 'tis night:
    when wood beasts creep out all.

21 After their prey young Lions roare:
    from God for food they call.

22 The Sun doth rise, then in their dennes
    they couch, when gone aside.

23 Man to his work & labour goes,
    untill the ev'ning-tide.

24 O Lord, how many are thy works!

in

all of them thou haſt wrought
in wiſdome: with thy plenteous ſtore
the earth is fully fraught.
25 So is this great & ſpatious ſea,
wherin things creeping bee
beyond all number: beaſts of ſmall
& of great quantitee.
25 There goe the ſhips: Leviathan
therin thou madſt to play.
27 Theſe all wayt on thee, that their meate
in their time give thou may.
28 They gather what thou giveſt them:
thy hand thou op'neſt wide,
& they with ſuch things as are good
are fully ſatiſfyde.
29 Thou hid'ſt thy face, they troubled are,
their breath thou tak'ſt away,
then doe they dye: alſo returne
unto their duſt doe they.
30 They are created, when thou makſt
thy ſpirit forth to go:
thou of the earth doſt make the face
to be renew'd alſo.
(4)
31 The glory of Iehovah ſhall
for evermore indure:
in his owne works Iehovah ſhall
joyfully take pleaſure.
32 The earth doth tremble, when that hee
upon the ſame doth look,
the mountaines he doth touch, likewiſe
Bb

they

201

they therupon do ſmoak.
14 Full ſweet my meditation
concerning him ſhall be:
ſo that I in Iehovah will
rejoyce *exceedinglee*.
35 *Let* ſinnets be conſum'd from th'earth,
& wicked be no more:
bleſſe thou Iehovah, o my ſoule,
prayſe yee the Lord *therefore*.

Pſalme 105.

O Prayſe the Lord, call on his Name.
'mong people ſhew his facts.
2 Sing unto him, ſing pſalmes to him:
talk of all's wondrous acts.
3 Let their hearts joy, that ſeek the Lord:
boaſt in his Holy-Name.
4 The Lord ſeek, & his ſtrengh: his face
alwayes ſeek yee *the ſame*.
5 Thoſe admirable works that hee
hath done remember you:
his wonders, & the judgements which
doe from his mouth *iſſue*.
6 O yee his ſervant Abrahams ſeed:
ſonnes of choſe Iacob yee.
7 He is the Lord our God: in all
the earth his judgements bee.
8 His Covenant for evermore,
and his comanded word,
a thouſand generations to
he doth in minde record,
9 Which he with Abraham made, and's oath

to

10 to Ifack. Made it faft,
  a law to Iacob: & Ifr'ell
    a Cov'nant aye to laft.

(2)

11 He fayd, I'le give thee Canans land:
    by lot, heirs to be there.
12 When few, yea very few in count
    and ftrangers in't they were;
13 When they did from one nation
    unto another pafs:
  when from one Kingdome their goings
    to other people was,
14 *He* fuffred none to doe them wrong:
    Kings checkt he for their fake:
15 Touch not mine oynted ones; none ill
    uhto my Prophets make.
16 He cal'd for Famine on the land,
    all ftaffe of bread brake hee.
17 Before them fent a man: Iofeph
    fold for a flave to bee.
18 *Whofe* feet they did with fetters hurt:
    in yr'n his foule did lye.
19 Vntill the time that his word came:
    the Lords word did him trye.
20 The King the peoples Ruler fent,
    loof'd him & let him go.
21 He made him Lord of all his houfe:
    of all's wealth ruler too:
22 At's will to binde his Peers: & teach
23 his Ancients fkill. Then came
  Ifr'ell to Egypt: & Iacob
            B b 2   fojourn'd

sojourn'd i'th land of Ham.

24 Hee much increaſt his folk: & made
them ſtronger then their foe,

25 Their heart he turn'd his folk to hate:
to's ſervants craft to ſhow.

(3)

25 Moſes his ſervant he did ſend:
& Aaron whom he choſe.

27 His ſignes & wonders them amongſt,
they in Hams land diſcloſe.

28 Hee darknes ſent, & made it dark:
nor did they's word gain-ſay.

29 Hee turn'd their waters into bloud:
& he their fiſh did ſlay.

30 Great ſtore of Frogs their land brought forth
in chambers of their Kings.

31 He ſpake,there came mixt ſwarmes,& lice
in all their coaſts *he brings.*

32 He gave them haile for raine: & in
their land fires flame did make.

33 And ſmote their Vines & their Figtrees:
& their coaſt-trees he brake.

34 He ſpake, & then the Locuſts came:
& Caterpillars, ſuch
the number of them was as none
could reckon up how much;

35 And ate all their lands herbs: & did
fruit of their ground devoure.

36 All firſt borne in their land he ſmote:
the chief of all their powre.

37 with

(4)

37 With silver also & with gold
    he them from thence did bring:
  & among all their tribes there was
    not any one weak-ling.

38 Egypt was glad when out they went:
    for on them fell their dread.

39 A cloud for cov'ring, & a fire
    to light the night he spred.

40 They askt, & he brought quailes: did them
    with heav'ns bread satiffy,

41 He op't the rock and waters flow'd:
    flouds ran in places dry.

42 For on his holy promise, bee
    and's servant Abraham thought.

43 With joye his people, and with songs
    forth he his chosen brought.

44 He of the heathen people did
    the land on them bestow:
  the labour of the people they
    inherited also:

45 To this intent that his statutes
    they might observe *alwayes:*
  also that they his lawes might keepe.
    doe yee Iehovah prayse.

Psalme 106.

PRayse yee the Lord, o to the Lord
   give thanks, for good is hee:
for his mercy continued is
    to perpetuitee.

2 Who can the Lords strong acts forth tell?

Bb 3

Or

or all his prayſe diſplay?
3 Bleſt they that judgement keep: & who
doth righteouſnes alway.
4 With favour of thy people, Lord,
doe thou remember mee:
and mee with that ſalvation
viſit which is of thee:
5 To ſee thy choſens good, to joy
in gladnes of thy nation:
that with thine owne inheritance
I might have exultation
6 As our fore-fathers ſo have wee
ſinned erroniouſly:
wee practiſ'd have iniquity,
wee have done wickedly.

(2)

7 Our fathers did not underſtand,
thy wonders in Egypt,
nor was thy mercyes multitude
in their remembrance kept:
But at the ſea at the red ſea
8 vext him. Yet for his owne
Names ſake he ſav'd them: that he might
his mighty powre make-knowne.
9 The red ſea alſo he rebuk't,
and dryed up it was:
ſo that as through the wildernes,
through depths he made them paſs.
10 And from the hand of him that did
them hate, he ſet them free:
and them redeemed from his hand

that

that was their enemee.
11 The waters covered their foes:
of them there was left none.
12 They did believe his word; they sang
his prayses therupon.

(3)

13 They soone forgot his words; nor would
they for his counsell stay:
14 But much i'th wildernes did lust;
i'th desart God tryde they.
15 And he their suite them gave; but sent
leannes their soule into.
16 They envi'd Moses in the camp,
Aaron Gods Saint also.
17 The opned earth, Dathan devour'd;
and hid Abirams troup.
18 And fire was kindled in their rout:
flame burnt the wicked up.
19 In *Horeb* made a calfe; also
molt image worshipt they.
20 They chang'd their glory to be like,
an oxe that eateth hay.
21 They God forgot their saviour, which
in Egipt did great acts:
22 *Works* wondrous in the land of *Ham*:
by th'red sea dreadfull facts.
23 And sayd, he would them waste; had not
Moses stood (whom he chose)
'fore him i'th breach, to turne his wrath,
lest that hee should waste *those*,

24 Yet

(4)

24 Yet they despis'd the pleasant land:
   nor did believe his word:

25 But murmur'd in their tents:the voyce
   they heard not of the Lord.

26 To make them fall i'th desart then,
   'gainst them he lift his hands.

27 'Mongst nations eke to fell their seed,
   and scatter them i'th lands.

28 And to Baal-Peor they joyn'd themselves:
   ate offrings of the dead.

29 Their works his wrath did thus provoake:
   the plague amongst them spread.

30 Then Phineas rose, & judgement did:
   and so the plague did stay.

31 Which justice to him counted was:
   to age and age for aye.

(5)

32 At th'waters of contention
   they angred him also:
   so that with Moses for their sakes,
   it *very* ill did go:

33 Because his spirit they provoakt:
   with's lips to speake rashly.

34 The nations as the Lord them charg'd,
   they stroyd not utterly:

35 But were amongst the Heathen mixt,
   and learn'd their works to do:

36 And did their Idols serve; which then
   became a snare unto.

37 Yea, unto divills, they their sonnes

and

and daughters offered.

38 And guiltlesse bloud, bloud of their sons
& of their daughters shed,
Whom unto Canans Idols they
offred in sacrifice :
the land with bloud abundantly
polluted was likewise.

39 Thus with the works were they defylde
which they themselves had done:
and they did goe a whoring with
inventions of their owne:

(6)

40 Therefore against his folk the wrath
was kindled of the Lord:
so that he the inheritance
which was his owne abhorr'd.

41 And he gave them to heathens hand;
their haters their lords were.

42 Their foes thral'd them; under their hand
made them the yoake to beare.

43 Oft he deliverd them; but they
provoakt him bitterly
with their counsell, & were brought low
for their iniquity.

44 Yet, he regarded their distresse;
when he did heare their plaint.

45 And he did to remembrance call
for them his Covenant:
And in his many mercyes did

46 repent. And made them bee
pitty'd of all that led them forth

Cc   into

into captivitee.

47 Save us, o Lord our God, & us
from heathens gath'ring rayse
to give thanks to thy Holy-Name:
to triumph in thy prayse.

48 The Lord the God of Israell
from aye to aye blest bee:
and let all people say Amen.
o prayse Iehovah yee.

THE

Fift Booke

Psalme 107.

O Give yee thanks unto the Lord,
because that good is hee:
because his loving kindenes lasts
to perpetuitee.

2 So let the Lords redeem'd say: whom
hee freed from th'enemies hands:

3 And gathred them from East, & *West*,
from South, & Northerne lands.

4 I'th desart, in a desart way
they wandred: no towne finde,

5 to dwell in. Hungry & thirsty:
their soule within them pinde.
Then did they to Iehovah cry
when they were in distresse:
who did them set at liberty

out

out of their anguishes.

7 In such a way that was most right
 he led them forth also:
that to a citty which they might
 inhabit they might go.

8 O that men would Iehovah prayse
 for his great goodnes *then*:
& for his workings wonderfull
 unto the sonnes of men.

9 Because that he the longing soule
 doth throughly satisfy:
the hungry soule he also fills
 with good abundantly.

(2)

10 Such as in darknes' and within
 the shade of death abide;
who are in sore affliction,
 also in yron tyde:

11 By reason that against the words
 of God they did rebell;
also of him that is most high
 contemned the counsell.

12 Therefore with molestation
 hee did bring downe their heart:
downe did they fall, & none their was
 could help to them impart.

13 Then did they to Iehovah cry
 when they were in distress:
who did them set at liberty
 out of their anguishes.

14 He did them out of darknes bring,

Cc 2   also

also deaths shade from under:
as for the bands that they were in
he did them break asunder.
15 O that men would Iehovah prayse
for his great goodnes then:
and for his workings wonderfull
unto the sonnes of men.
15 For he hath all to shivers broke
the gates that were of brasse:
& hee asunder cut each barre
that made of yron was.

(3)

17 For their transgressions & their sins,
fooles doe affliction beare.
18 All kinde of meate their soule abhorrest
to deaths gate they draw neare.
19 Then did they to Iehovah cry
when they were in distress:
who did them set at liberty
out of their anguishes.
20 He, sent his word, & therewithall
healing to them he gave:
from out of their destructions
he did them also save.
21 O that men would Iehovah prayse,
for his great goodnes then:
& for his workings wonderfull
unto the sons of men.
22 And sacrifices sacrifice
let them of thanksgiving:
& while his works they doe declare

let

let them for gladnes sing.

(4)

23 They that goe downe to'th sea in ships:
   their busines there to doo

24 in waters great. The Lords work see,
   it'h deep his wonders too.

25 Because that he the stormy winde
   commandeth to arise:
   which lifteth up the waves therof,

26 They mount up to the skyes:
   Downe goe they to the depths againe,
   their soule with ill doth quaile.

27 They reele,& stagger,drunkard like,
   and all their wirt doth faile.

28 Then did they to Iehovah cry
   when they were in distress:
   and therupon he bringeth them
   out of their anguishes.

29 Hee makes the storme a calme: so that
   the waves therof are still.

30 Their rest then glads them; he them brings
   to'th hav'n which they did will.

31 O that men would Iehovah prayse
   for his great goodnes them:
   & for his workings wonderfull
   unto the sons of men.

32 Also within the peoples Church
   him let them highly rayse:
   where Elders are assembled,there
   him also let them prayse.

Cc 2   33 Hee

(5)

33 He rivers to a defart turnes,
 to drought the springing well:
34 A fruitfull foyle to barrennes;
 for their fin there that dwell.
35 The defart to a poole he turnes;
 and dry ground to a fpring.
36 Seates there the hungry; who prepare
 their towne of habiting,
37 Vineyards there alfo for to plant,
 alfo to fow the field;
which may unto them fruitfull things
 of much revenue yield.
38 Alfo he bleffeth them, fo that
 they greatly are increaft:
and for to be diminifhed
 he fuffers not their beaft:
39 Againe they are diminifhed
 & they are brought downe low;
by reafon of their preffing-ftreights,
 affliction & forrow.

(6)

40 On Princes he contempt doth powre;
 and caufeth them to ftray
i'th folitary wildernes,
 wherin there is no way.
41 Yet hee out of affliction
 doth make the poore to rife:
& like as if it were a flock
 doth make him families.
42 The righteous fhall it behold,

and

and he shall joyfull bee:
in silence stop her mouth also
shall all iniquitee.

43 Who so is wise, & who so will
these things attentive learne:
the loving kindenes of the Lord
they clearely shall discerne.

Psalme 108.

A song or psalme of David.

O GOD, my heart's fixt, l'le sing;prayse
sing ev'n with my glory.
2 Awake thou Psaltery & Harp;
I will awake early.
3 O thou Iehovah, thee will I
the people prayse among:
within the midst of nations
thee will I prayse with song.
4 For o're the heav'ns thy mercys great;
to'th skyes thy truth doth mount.
5 Or'e heav'ns o God, be lift, all earth
let thy glory surmount:
6 That thy beloved people may
be set at libertee:
with thy right hand salvation give,
& doe thou answer mee.

(2)

7 God hath in his *owne* holines
spoken, rejoyce I shall:
of Shechem I'le division make;
& mete out Succoths vale.
8 Mine Gilead, mine Manasseh is,

and

& Ephraim also hee
is of my head the strength: Iudah
  shall my law-giver bee.
9 Moab my wash-pot, I will cast
  over Edom my shoo:
I'le make a shout triumphantly
  over Philistia too.
10 Who is it that will bring me to
  the citty fortifyde?
who is it that into Edom
  will be to mee a guide?
11 Wilt not thou doe this thing, o God,
  who didst us cast thee fro?
& likewise wilt not thou o God,
  forth with our armies go?
12 From trouble give us help; for vaine
  is mans salvation.
13 Through God wee shall do valiantly;
  for hee'l our foes tread downe.

Psalme 109.

To the chief musician, a psalme
  of David.

GOD of my prayse, hold not thy peace,
  For mouth of the wicked,
& mouth of the deceitfull are
  against mee opened:
Gainst mee they speake with lying tongue.
5   And compasse mee about
with words of hate; & mee against
  without a cause they fought.
4 They for my love mine enemies are:

                                    but

but I my prayer make.

5 And ill for good rewarded mee;
　　& hate for my loves sake.

6 A wicked person over him
　　doe thou make for to sit,
also at his right hand doe thou
　　let Satan stand at it.

7 When he is judged, let him then
　　condemned be therin:
and let the prayr that bee doth make.
　　be turned into sin.

8 Few let his dayes bee: & let his
　　office another take.

9 His children let be fatherlesse,
　　and's wife a widow make.

10 Let's children still be vagabonds,
　　begge they their bread also;
out of their places desolate
　　let them a seeking go.

(2)

11 Yea, let th'extortioner catch all
　　that doth to him pertaine:
and let the stranger spoyle what he
　　did by his labour gaine.

12 Let there not any bee that may
　　mercy to him expresse:
nor any one that favour may
　　his children fatherlesse.

13 The issue also let thou be
　　cut off that from him came:
it'h following generation

D

our

out blotted be his name.

14 Remembred with the Lord be his
    fathers iniquitee:
  and of his mother never let
    the sin out blotted bee.

15 Before Iehovah let them bee
    continually put:
  that from out of the earth he may
    the mem'ry of them cut.

16 Becaufe that he remembred not
    compaffion to impart,
  but did purfue the needy poore:
    to flay the broke in heart.

(3)

17 As he did curfing love, fo let
    curfing unto him come:
  as he did not in bleffing joy,
    fo be it far him from.

18 With curfing like a robe as hee
    cloath'd him: fo let it go
  like water to his bowels, and
    like oyle his bones into.

19 Garment like let it to him be,
    himfelfe for to aray:
  and for a girdle, wherewith hee
    may gird himfelfe alway.

20 Thus let mine adverfaryes bee
    rewarded from the Lord:
  alfo of them againft my foule
    that fpeak an evil word,

21 **But**

(4)

21 But God the Lord, for thy Names sake,
o doe thou well for mee:
because thy mercy it is good,
o doe thou set mee free.

22 For poore & needy I: in mee
my heart's wounded also.

23 Like falling shade I passe: I 'me tost
Locust like to & fro.

24 Through fasts my knees are weak: my flesh
it's fatnes doth forsake.

25 And I am their reproach: they look
at mee, their heads they shake.

26 Help mee, o Lord my God: after
thy mercy save thou mee:

27 That they may know this is thy hand:
Lord that it's done by thee.

28 Let them curse, but o doe thou blesse;
when as that they arise
let them be shamed, thy servant
let him rejoyce likewise.

29 Mine adversaryes o let them
with shame be cloath'd upon:
& themselves cloath as with a cloak
with their confusion.

30 I'le to Iehovah with my mouth
give thanks exceedingly:
yea him among the multitude
with prayse I'le glorify.

31 For hee shall stand at right hand of
the poore & needy one:

Dd 2

from

from thofe that doe condemne his foule
to give falvation.
Pfalme 110.
A pfalme of David.

THe Lord did fay unto my Lord,
   fit thou at my right hand:
till I thine enemies make a ftoole
   wheron thy feet may ftand.

2 The Lord the rod fhall of thy ftrength
   fend from out of Sion:
in middeft of thine enemies
   have thou dominion.

3 Willing thy folk in thy dayes powre,
   in holy beautyes bee:
from mornings womb; thou haft the dew
   of thy youth unto thee.

4 Iehovah fware, nor will repent,
   thou art a Prieft for aye:
after the order that I of
   Melchizedeck did fay.

5 The Lord who is at thy right hand,
   wounding fhall ftrike through Kings
in that fame day wherin that hee
   his indignation brings.

6 Hee fhall among the heathen judge,
   and fill with bodies dead
great places, & o're many lands
   he fhall ftrike through the head.

7 Out of the torrent he fhall drink
   i'th way *hee paffeth by*:
becaufe of this therefore hee fhall

lift

lift up his head on hye.

Pfalme iii.

PRayfe yee the Lord: with my whole heart
Iehovah prayfe will I:
i'th private meetings of th'upright,
and publicke affembly.

2 Great are the Lords works: fought of all
that in them have pleafure.

3 Comely & glorious is his work:
aye doth his juftice dure.

4 To be remembred he hath made
his doings merveilous:
full of compaffion is the Lord
as well as gracious.

5 Meate hath hee given unto them
that fearers of him bee:
he evermore his covenant
doth keepe in memoree:

6 The power of his works hee did
unto his people fhow:
that he the heathens heritage
upon them might beftow.

(2)

7 Both verity & judgement are
the working of his hands:
yea very faithfull alfo are
each one of his commands.

8 For ever & for evermore
they ftand in ftablenes:
yea they are done in verity
alfo in uprightnes.

Dd i

9 Redemption

9 Redemption to his folk he sent,
    that covenant of his
for aye he hath ordaind: holy
    and reverend his Name is.
10 Of wisdome the begining is
    Iehovahs feare : all they
that doe his will have prudence good:
    his prayse indures for aye.

Psalme 112.

PRayse yee the *Lord*. blest is the man
    that doth Iehovah feare,
that doth in his commandements
    his spirit greatly cheare.
2 The *very* mighty upon earth
    shall be that are his seed:
they also shall be blessed that
    from th' upright doe proceed.
3 And there shall be within his house
    both wealth & much rich store:
his righteousnes it also doth
    indure for evermore.
4 In midst of darknes there doth light
    to upright ones arise:
both gracious, & pittyfull,
    righteous he is likewise.

(2)

5 A good man hee doth favour show
    & ready is to lend:
and with descretion his affayres
    he carryes to an end.
6 That man shall not assuredly

fos

for ever moved bee:
the righteous man he shall be had
in lasting memoree.

7 By evill tydings that he heares
he shall not be afrayd:
his trust he putting in the Lord.
his heart is firmly stayd.

8 His heart is sure established,
feare shall not him surprise,
untill he see what hee desires
upon his enemies.

9 He hath disperst, hath giv'n to poore:
his justice constantly
indureth: & his horne shall be
with honour lifted hye.

10 The wicked shall see, & be griev'd;
gnash with his teeth shall hee
and melt away: and their desire
shall faile that wicked bee.

Psalme 113.

THe Lord prayse yee, prayse yee the Lord
his servants Gods Name prayse.

2 O blessed be Iehovahs Name,
from henceforth & alwayes.

3 From rising to the setting sun:
the Lords Name's to be praysd.

4 The Lord all nations is above:
o're heav'ns his glory raysd

5 Who is like to, the Lord our God?
who upon earth doth dwell.

6 Who humble doth himselfe to view.

in

in heav'n, in earth as well.
7 The needy from the duſt he lifts:
the poore lifts from the dung.
8 That hee with princes may him ſet:
his peoples *Peeres* among.
9 The barren woman he doth make
to keepe houſe, & to bee
a joyfull mother of children:
wherefore the Lord prayſe yee.

Pſalme 114.

VVHen Iſrell did depart
th'Egyptians from among,
and Iacobs houſe from a people
that were of a ſtrange tongue:
2 Iudah his holy place:
Iſrell's dominion was.
3 The ſea it ſaw, & fled: Iordane
was forced back to paſs.
4 The mountaines they did leap
upwards like unto rams:
the litle hills alſo they did
leap up like unto lambs.
5 Thou ſea what made thee flye?
thou Iordane, back to go?
6 Yee mountaines that yee ſkipt like rams:
like lambs yee hills alſo?
7 Earth at Gods preſence dread,
at Iacobs Gods preſence:
8 The rock who turnes to waters lake:
ſprings he from flint ſends thence.

Pſalme

PSALME Cxv.

NOt to us, nor unto us, Lord,
    but glory to thy Name afford:
  for thy mercy, for thy truths ſake.
2 The heathen wherefore ſhould they ſay:
where is their God now gone away?
3   But heavn's our God his ſeat doth make:
Hee hath done whatſoe're he would.
4 Their Idols are ſilver & gold:
    the handy work of men they were.
5 Mouths have they, ſpeachleſſe yet they bee:
eyes have they, but they doe not ſee.
6   eares have they but they doe not heare:
Noſes have they, but doe not ſmell.
7 Hands have they, but cannot handell,
    feet have they but they doe not go:
And through their throat they never ſpake.
8 Like them are they, that doe them make:
    & all that truſt in them are ſo.
9 Truſt in the Lord o Iſraell,
he is their help, their ſhield as well.
10   O Arons houſe the Lord truſt yee:
Hee is their help,& hee their ſhield.
11 Who feare the Lord, truſt to him yield:
    their help alſo their ſhield is hee.

(2)

12 The Lord hath mindefull been of us,
he'le bleſſe us, he'le bleſſe iſr'ells houſe:
    bleſſing he'le Arons houſe afford.
13 He'le bleſſe Gods fearers: great & ſmall.
14 You & your ſons, the Lord much ſhall

        Ee   increaſe

15 increase still. You blest of the Lord
16 which heav'n & earth made. Heav'ns heav'ns.
the Lords: but th'earth mens sons gives hee. (bee
17 The Lords prayse dead doe not afford:
Nor any that to silence bow.
13 But wee will blesse the Lord both now
      and ever henceforth. prayse the Lord

Psalme 116.

I Love the Lord, because he doth
    my voice & prayer heare.
2 And in my dayes will call, because
    he bow'd to mee his eare.
3 The pangs of death on ev'ry side
    about beset mee round:
the paines of hell 'gate hold on mee,
    distresse & griefe I found.
4 Vpon Iehovahs Name therefore
    I called, & did say,
deliver thou my soule, o Lord,
    I doe thee humbly pray.
5 Gracious the Lord & just, our God
    is mercifull also.
6 The Lord the simple keeps: & hee
    sav'd mee when I was low.
7 O thou my soule doe thou returne
    unto thy quiet rest:
because the Lord to thee himselfe
    hath bounteously exprest.
8 For thou hast freed my soule from death,
    mine eyes from teares, from fall
9 my feet, Before the Lord i'th land

of

of living walk I shall.

(2)

10 I did believe, therefore I spake:
 afflicted much was I.

11 That every man a lyar is
 I did say hastily.

12 What shall I render to the Lord,
 to mee for's benefits all.

13 I'le take the cup of saving health
 & on the Lords Name call.

14 In presence now of all his folk,
 I'le pay the Lord my vowes.

15 Of his Saints, in Iehovahs sight
 the death is pretious.

16 I am thy servant, truly Lord
 thine owne servant am I:
 I am the son of thy hand-maide,
 my bands thou didst untye.

17 Of thankfgiving the sacrifice
 offer to thee I will:
 Iehovahs Name I earneftly
 will call upon it ftill.

18 Vnto Iehovah I will pay
 the vowes were made by mee,
now in the presence of all them
 that his owne people bee.

19 Within the Courts of the Lords house,
 ev'n in the midft of thee
 o thou *citty* Ierufalem:
 o prayfe Iehovah yee.

Pfalme 117.

E e 2

PSALM

PSALM C xvii, C xviii.

AL nations, prayſe the Lord; him prayſe
all people. For his mercies bee
great toward us: alſo alwayes
the Lords truth laſts. the Lord prayſe yee.

Another of the ſame.

AL nations, prayſe the Lord; all folk
prayſe him. For his mercee
is great to us; & the Lords truth
aye iaſts. the Lord prayſe yee.

Pſalme 118.

O Give yee thanks unto the Lord,
becauſe that good is hee;
becauſe his loving kindenes laſts
to perpetuitee.

2 For ever that his mercie laſts
let Iſraell now ſay.

3 Let Arons houſe now ſay, that his
mercie indures for aye.

4 Likewiſe let them now ſay, who of
Iehovah fearers bee;
his loving kindenes that it laſts
to perpetuitee.

5 I did lift up my voice to God
from out of ſtreitnes great;
the Lord mee anſwerd, & mee plac't
in an inlarged ſeat.

6 The Lord's for mee, I will not feare
what man can doe to mee.

7 Iehovah takes my part with them
that of mee helpers bee;
Therefore upon them that mee hate

my

my wishes see shall I.

8 'Tis better to trust in the Lord:
   then on man to rely.

(2)

9 'Tis better to trust on the Lord:
   then trust in Princes put.

10 All nations compast mee, but them
   in Gods Name I'le off cut.

11 They compast mee about, yea they
   mee compassed about:
  but in Iehovahs Name I will
   them utterly root out.

12 They compast mee like Bees, are quencht
   like as of thornes the flame:
  but I will utterly destroy
   them in Iehovahs Name.

13 Thou didst thrust sore to make mee fall:
   the Lord yet helped mee.

14 The Lord my fortitude & song:
   & saving health is hee.

15 The tabernacles of the just
   the voice of joye afford
  & of salvation: strongly works
   the right hand of the Lord.

16 The right hand of Iehovah is
   exalted up on hye:
  the right hand of Iehovah is
   a working valiantly.

(3)

17 I shall not dye, but live: & tell
   what things the Lord worketh.

E e 3   18 The

PSALM C XVIII.

18 The Lord did forely chaſten mee:
　　but gave mee not to death.
19 O ſet wide open unto mee
　　the gates of righteouſnes:
　I will goe into them, & will
　　Iehovahs praiſe confeſs.
20 This ſame Iehovahs gate at which
　　the juſt ſhall enter in.
21 I'le praiſe thee, for thou haſt mee heard,
　　and haſt my ſafety bin.
22 The ſtone which builders did refuſe
　　head corner ſtone now lyes.
23 This is the doing of the Lord:
　　it's wondrous in our eyes,

(4)

24 This is the very day the which
　　Iehovah hee hath made:
　wee will exceedingly rejoyce,
　　& in it will be glad.
25 Iehovah I doe thee beſeech,
　　ſalvation now afford:
　I humbly thee intreat, now ſend
　　proſperity, o Lord.
26 Hee that comes in Iehovahs Name
　　o let him bleſſed bee:
　out of Iehovahs houſe to you
　　a bleſſing with doe wee.
27 God he Iehovah is, and hee
　　light unto us affords:
　the ſacrifices binde unto
　　the altars hornes with cords.

Thou

28 Thou art my God, & I'le thee prayse,
   my God I'le set thee hye.
29 O prayse the Lord, for he is good,
   and aye lasts his mercy.

Psalme 119.

N (1) Aleph
ALL-blest are men upright of way:
   walk in Iehovahs law who do.
2 Blest such as doe his records keepe:
   with their whole heart him seek also.
3 And that work no iniquitie:
   but in his wayes doe walke *indeed.*
4 Thou hast giv'n charge, with diligence
   unto thy precepts to give heed.
5 Ah that to keepe thy statutes: so
   my wayes addressed were by thee.
6 When I respect thy precepts all,
   then shall I not ashamed bee.
7 Whē Ithy righteous judgements learne
   with hearts uprightnes I'le thee prayse.
8 Forsake thou mee not utterly:
   I will observe thy statute-wayes.

B ב (2) Beth
9 By what may ' young man cleanse his way?
   by heeding it as thy word guides.
10 With my whole heart thee have I sought:
   thy lawes let mee not goe besides.
11 I in my heart thy word have hid:
   that I might not against thee sin.
12 Thou o Iehovah, blessed art:
   thine owne statutes instruct mee in.

13 All

23 All the just judgements of thy mouth
    declared with my lips have I.

24 I in thy testimonyes way
    joy more then in all rich plenty.

15 In thy precepts I'le meditate:
    and have respect unto thy wayes.

16 My selfe I'le solace in thy lawes:
    and not forget what thy word *sayes*.

(3)   Gimel

17 Confer this grace thy servant to,
    that I may live thy word to keep.

13 Vnveile mine eyes, that I may see
    out of thy law the wonders *sleep*.

19 I am a stranger in the earth:
    do not thy precepts from me hide.

20 My soule is broken with desire
    unto thy judgements time & tide.

21 Thou hast rebuk'd the proud, acurst
    which doe frō thy commandments swerve.

22 Roll off from mee reproach & scorne:
    for I thy records doe observe.

23 Ev'n Princes sate & 'gainst mee spake;
    but on thy lawes thy servant mus'd.

24 Thy records also are my joyes:
    and for men of my counsell *us'd*.

(4)   Daleth

25 Downe to the dust my soule cleav's fast:
    o quicken mee after thy word.

26 I show'd my wayes & thou mee heardst:
    thy statutes learning mee afford.

27 Thy precepts way make mee to know:

so

ſo I'le muſe on thy wondrous wayes.

28 My ſoule doth melt for heavines:
according to thy word mee rayſe.

29 The way of lying from mee take;
and thy law grant mee graciouſly.

30 The way of truth I choſen have:
thy judgements *fore mee* layd have I.

31 Thy teſtimonies cleave I to;
o Lord, on mee ſhame do not caſt.

32 Then ſhall I run thy precepts way,
when thou mine heart enlarged haſt.

E꜖ (5) He.

33 Enforme mee Lord, in thy laws path;
and I will keep it to the end.

34 Skill give mee, & thy law I'le keep:
yea with my whole heart it attend.

35 Cauſe mee to tread thy precepts path;
becauſe therin delight I do.

36 Vnto thy records bend my heart;
& covetouſnes not unto.

37 From vaine ſights turne away mine eyes:
and in thy way make mee to live.

38 Confirme thy word thy ſervant to,
who to thy feare himſelfe doth give.

39 My ſlander which I feare remove;
becauſe thy judgements good they bee.

40 Loe for thy precepts I have lon'gd:
o in thy juſtice quicken mee.

F꜖ (6) Vau.

41 Finde mee out let thy mercies Lord:
thy ſaving health as thou haſt ſayd.

F f

42 Sc

233

43 So I my taunters answer shall,
for on thy word my hope is stayd.

43 Nor truths-word quite frō my mouth take:
because thy.judgements I attend.

44 So I thy law shall alway keep,
to everlasting without end.

45 And I will walk at libertie,
because I doe thy precepts seek.

46 Nor will I blush, when before Kings
I of thy testimonies speak.

47 In thy commands, which I have lov'd,
also my selfe delight I will.

48 And lift my hands to thy commands
belov'd: & minde thy statutes still.

(7) Sajin.

49 Good to thy servant make the word,
on which to hope thou didst mee give.

50 This was my comfort in my griefe,
because thy word doth make mee live.

51 The proud have much derided mee:
yet have I not thy law declinde.

52 Thy judgements Lord, that are of old,
I did recall, & comfort finde.

53 Horrour hath taken hold on mee:
for lewd men that thy law forsake.

54 I, in my pilgrimages house,
of thy statutes my songs doe make.

55 By night remembred I thy Name,
o Lord: & I thy law observe.

56 This hath been unto mee, because
I from thy precepts did not swerve.

Hee

H Π (8) Heth.

57 Hee, ev'n the Lord, my portion is,
I said that I would keep thy word.

58 With my whole heart thy face I begg'd:
thy promis'd mercies mee afford.

59 I thought upon my waies, & turn'd
my feet into thy testaments.

60 I hasted, & made no delaies
to keepe with heed thy commandments.

61 The bands of wicked men mee robb'd:
of thy law I am not mindeless.

62 Ile rise at midnight thee to praise;
for judgements of thy righteousnes.

63 Companion am I to all them,
that feare thee, & thy laws doe heed.

64 Thy mercie fills the earth, o Lord:
teach mee the lawes thou hast decreed.

I ☐ (9) Teth.

65 Iehovah, with thy servant thou
after thy word, right-well hast done.

66 Good taste & knowledge, teach thou mee,
for I believe thy precepts on.

67 Before I was chastis'd, I stray'd:
but I thy word observ'd have now.

68 Thou art good, & art doing good:
thy statutes teach mee, oh doe thou.

69 The proud against mee forg'd a lye:
thy laws I'le keepe with my hearts-might.

70 The heart of them is fat as grease:
but in thy law I doe delight.

71 It's good for mee, I was chastis'd:

Ff 2

that

that so thy statutes learne I should.

72 Better to mee is thy mouths-law,
    then thousands of silver & gold.

(10)   Iod.

73 Know make mee, & I'le learn thy lawes:
    thy hands mee formed have, & made.

74 Who feare thee, mee shall see, & joy:
    because hope in thy word I had.

75   Thy judgements Lord, I know are just;
    & faithfully thou chastnedst mee.

76 As thou hast to thy servant spoke,
    now let thy grace my comfort bee.

77   Send mee thy grace, that I may live;
    for thy law as my joy I chuse.

78 Shame proud ones, that mee falsly wrong:
    but I will in thy precepts muse.

79   Let them that feare thee turne to mee;
    and such as have thy records knowne.

80 Let my heart bee in thy lawes found
    that so I shame may suffer none.

(11)   Caph.

81 Look for thy word I doe, *when as*
    my soule doth faint for help from thee

82 Mine eies have failed for thy word,
    saying, when wilt thou comfort mee?

83   I like a smoake-dride-bottle am;
    yet doe I not thy laws forgoe.

84 what are thy servants daies? when wilt
    on my pursuers judgement doe?

85   The proud have digged pits for mee,
    which doe not unto thy law sute.

All

86 All thy comands are truth: help mee,
  they wrongfully mee perfecute.

87   They nigh had wafted mee on earth,
  but I thy laws did not forfake.

88 To keep the records of thy mouth,
  mee in thy mercie lively make.

  M ז   (12)   Lamed.
89 Made faft i'th heavens is thy word,
  o Lord, for ever to endure.

90 From age to age thy faithfullnes:
  thou form'dft the earth, & it ftands-fure.

91   As thou ordain'dft, they ftill abide;
  for all are fervants thee unto.

92 Had not thy law been my delight:
  Then had I perifht in my wo.

93   Thy ftatutes I will ne're forget:
  becaufe by them thou quicknedft mee.

94 Thine owne am I, fave mee, becaufe
  I fought thy precepts ftudiouflee.

95   The wicked watch mee, mee to ftroy:
  but I thy teftimonies minde.

96 Of all perfection, end I fee:
  but very large thy law *I finde.*

  N נ   (13)   Mem.
97 Now how much doe I love thy law?
  it is my ftudy all the day.

98 Thou mad'ft mee wifer then my foes
  by thy rule: for it's with mee aye.

99   I'me wifer then my teachers all:
  for thy records my ftudy are.

100 I more then ancients underftand;
    Ff 3   becaufe

because I kept thy laws with care.

101   From each ill path my feet I stay'd:
that so I might thy word obserue.

102 Because thou hast instructed mee,
I did not from thy judgements swerue.

103   How sweet are thy words to my taste?
to my mouth more then honie they.

104 I from thy precepts wisdome learne:
therefore I hate each lying way.

O   ℶ (14)   Nun.

105   Of my feet is thy word the lamp:
and to my path the shining light.

106 Sworne haue I, & will it performe,
that I will keep thy judgements right.

107   I am afflicted very much:
Lord quicken mee after thy word.

108 Accept my mouths free-offrings now:
& mee thy judgements teach o Lord.

109   My soule is alwaies in my hand:
but I haue not thy law forgot.

110 The wicked laide for mee a snare:
yet from thy laws I strayed not.

111   Thy recods are mine heritage
for aye: for my hearts joy they bee.

112 I bent my heart still to performe
thy statues to eternitee.

P   ם (15)   Samech.

113   Pursue-I doe with hatred, all
vaine thoughts: but love thy law doe:

114 My covert & my shield art thou:
I on thy word wait hopefully.

115 Depart from mee, lewd men, that I
may keepe my Gods commandements.

116 By thy word ſtay mee, & I live:
nor ſhame mee for my confidence.

117 Suſteine mee, & I ſhall be ſafe:
and in thy law ſtill I'le delight.

118 thou tread'ſt downe all that from thy laws
doe ſtray: for falſe is their deceit.

119 All th'earths lewd ones like droſſe thou
therefore thy records love I do.   (ſtroyd'ſt

120 For feare of thee my fleſh doth quake:
I doe thy judgements dread alſo.

Q ÿ (16) Hajin.

121 uite to oppreſſors leave mee not:
I judgement doe, & righteouſnes.

122 thy ſervants ſuretie be for good:
let not the proud ones mee oppreſs.

123 Mine eyes for thy ſalvation faile:
as alſo for thy righteous word.

124 In mercie with thy ſervant deale:
& thy lawes-learning mee afford.

125 I am thy ſervant, make mee wiſe,
thy teſtimonies for to know.

126 Time for thee Lord it is to work,
for men thy law doe overthrow.

127 Therefore doe I thy precepts love
above gold, yea the fineſt gold.

128 All falſe paths hate I: for thy rules
of all things, are all right, I hold.

R Đ (17) Pe.

129 ight-wondrous are thy teſtimonies:

there

239

therefore my soule keeps them with care.

150 The entrance of thy words gives light:
and makes them wise that simple are.

151   I gape & pant for thy precepts;
because I longed *for the same*.

152 Look on mee, & such grace mee show,
as thou dost them that love thy Name.

153   My steps by thy word guide: & let
no wickednes beare rule in mee.

154 From mens oppression mee redeem:
and thy laws-keeper will I bee.

155   Make thy face on thy servant shine:
and mee to learne thy statutes cause.

156 Mine eies run floods of waters downe:
because they doe not keep thy laws.

S̈   (18)   Tzade.

157 Sincerely-just art thou, o Lord,
thy judgements upright are also.

158 Thy testimonies thou commandst
are right, yea, very faithfull too.

159   My zeale consumed mee, because
mine enemies thy words forget.

160 Thy word it is exceeding pure:
therefore thy servant loveth it.

161   Small am I, & contemptible:
yet thy commands forget not I.

162 Thy justice, justice is for aye:
also thy law is verity.

163   Distresse & anguish seas'd on mee:
yet thy commands delights mee give.

164 Thy records justice lasts for aye:

also

PSALME CxIx.

make thou mee wise, & I shall live.

Ꝓ (19) Koph.

145 To mee that cry with my whole heart
Lord heare: thy statutes keep I will.
146 I unto thee did cry: save mee,
& I shall keep thy records still.
147 The dawning I prevent, & cry:
I for thy word doe hopefull-waite.
148 Mine eyes prevent the night-watches,
in thy word for to meditate.

149 Lord, of thy mercy heare my voice:
after thy judgements quicken mee.
150 Who follow mischiefe, they draw nigh:
who from thy law afarre off bee.
151 But o Iehovah, thou art neere:
and all thy precepts verity.
152 I long since of thy records knew:
thou laid'st them for eternity.

ꞅ (20) Resch.

153 View mine affliction, & mee free:
for I thy law doe not forget.
154 Plead thou my cause, & mee redeem:
for thy words sake alive mee set.
155 Salvation from lewd men is far:
sith they thy laws to finde ne're strive.
156 Great are thy bowell- mercies Lord:
after thy judgements mee revive.

157 Many my foes and hunters are:
yet I not from thy records swerve.
158 I saw transgressors, & was griev'd,
for they thy word doe not observe.

Gg

See

159   See Lord, that I thy precepts love:
graunt, of thy bounty live I may.

160 Thy word's beginning it is truth:
and all thy right judgements for aye.

VV ַ [ )] . (21)   Schin.

161   ithout cause Princes mee pursue:
but of thy word my hearts in awe.

162 As one that hath much booty found,
so I rejoyce doe in thy law.

163   Lying I hate, & it abhorre:
but thy law dearly love doe I.

164 Seven times a day I prayse thee, for
the judgements of thine equity.

165   Great peace have they that love thy law:
& such shall finde no stumbling-stone.

166 I hop't for thy salvation, Lord:
and thy commandments I have done.

167   My soule thy testimonies keeps:
and them I love exceedinglee.

168 I keep thy rules & thy records:
for all my waies before thee bee.

Y ֹ ת (22)   Thau.

169   ield Lord, my cry, t'approach thy face:
as thou hast spoke, mee prudent make.

170 Let my request before thee come:
deliver mee for thy words sake.

171   My lips shall utter forth *thy* prayse:
when thou thy lawes hast learned mee.

172 My tongue shall forth thy word resound:
for all thy precepts justice *bee.*

173 To help mee let thy hand be neere:

foꝛ

for thy commandments chose have I.
174 I long for thy salvation, Lord:
and my delights in thy law ly.
175   Let my soule live, & shew thy prayse:
help mee also thy judgements let.
176 Like lost sheep strayd, thy servant seeke:
for I thy laws doe not forget

Psalme 120.
A song of degrees.

Vnto the Lord, in my distresse
  I cry'd, & he heard mee.
2 From lying lipps & guilefull tongue,
  o Lord, my soule set free.
3 What shall thy false tongue give to thee,
  or what on thee confer?
4 Sharp arrows of the mighty ones,
  with coales of juniper.
5 Woe's mee, that I in Mesech doe
  a sojourner remaine:
that I doe dwell in tents, which doe
  to Kedar appertaine.
6 Long time my soule hath dwelt with him
  that peace doth much abhorre,
7 I am for peace, but when I speake,
  they ready are for warre.

Psalme 121.
A song of degrees.

I To the hills lift up mine eyes,
  from whence shall come mine aid
2 Mine help doth from Iehovah come,
  which heav'n & earth hath made.

Gg 3   3 Hee

3 Hee will not let thy foot be mov'd,
    nor slumber; that thee keeps.
4 Loe hee that keepeth Israell,
    hee slumbreth not, nor sleeps.
5 The Lord thy keeper is, the Lord
    on thy right hand the shade.
6 The Sun by day, nor Moone by night,
    shall thee by stroke *invade.*
7 The Lord will keep the from all ill:
    thy soule hee keeps alway,
8 Thy going out, & thy income,
    the Lord keeps now & aye.

Psalme 122.
A song of degrees.

I Ioy'd in them, that to mee sayd
    to the Lords house go wee.
2 Ierusalem, within thy gates,
    our feet shall standing bee.
3 Ierusalem, it builded is
    like unto a citty
    together which compacted is
    within it selfe closely.
4. Whether the tribes, Gods tribes ascend
    unto Isr'ells witnes;
    that they unto Iehovahs Name
    may render thankfullnes.
5 For there the judgements thrones, the thrones
    of Davids house doe sit.
6 O for Ierusalem her peace
    see that yee pray for it:
    Prosper they shall that doe theelove.

7 peace

7   Peace in thy fortreſſes
     o let there be,proſperity
       within thy Pallaces.
8 For my brethren & for my friends,
     I'le now ſpeake peace to thee.
9 I'le for our God Iehovahs houſe,
     ſeek thy felicitee.

Pſalme 123.
A ſong of degrees.

O Thou that ſitteſt in the heav'ns,
    I lift mine eyes to thee.
2 Loe, as the ſervants eyes unto
     hand of their maſters bee:
   As maides eyes to her miſtreſſe hand,
     ſo are our eyes unto
   the Lord our God, untill that hee
     ſhall mercy to us ſhow.
3 O Lord be mercifull to us,
     mercifull to us bee:
   becauſe that filled with contempt
     exceedingly are wee.
4 With ſcorne of thoſe that be at eaſe,
     our ſoule's fill'd very much:
   alſo of thoſe that great ones are,
     ev'n with contempt of ſuch.

Pſalme 124.
A ſong of degrees. of David.

H Ad not the Lord been on our ſide,
    may Iſraell now ſay,
2 Had not God been for us,when men
     did riſe againſt us they:

                Gg 3   4 The

3 They had then swallow'd us alive,
　　when their wrath on us burn'd.
4 Then had the waters us o'rewhelmd,
　　the streame our soule or'e turnd.
5 The proud waters then, on our soule
　　had passed on their way:
6 Blest be the Lord, that to their teeth
　　did not give us a prey.
7 Our soule, as bird, escaped is
　　out of the fowlers snare:
　the snare asunder broken is,
　　and wee delivered are.
8 The succour which wee doe injoye,
　　is in Iehovahs Name:
　who is the maker of the earth,
　　and of the heavens frame.

psalme 125.

A song of degrees.

THey that doe in Iehovah trust
　　shall as mount Sion bee:
　which cannot be remo'vd, but shall
　　remaine perpetuallee.
2 Like as the mountaines round about
　　Ierusalem doe stay:
　so doth the Lord surround his folk,
　　from henceforth ev'n for aye.
3 For lewd mens rod on just mens lot
　　it shall not resting bee:
　lest just men should put forth their hand
　　unto iniquitee.
4 To those Iehovah, that be good,

gladnes

gladnes to them impart:
as also unto them that are
upright within their heart.
5 But who turne to their crooked wayes,
the Lord shall make them go
with workers of iniquity:
but peace be Isr'ell to.

psalme 126.
A song of degrees.

WHen as the Lord return'd againe
Sions captiviree:
at that time unto them that dreame
compared might wee bee.
2 Then was our mouth with laughter fill'd,
with singing then our tongue:
the Lord hath done great things for them
said they, t'heathens among.
3 The Lord hath done great things for us,
wherof wee joyfull bee.
4 As streames in South, doe thou o Lord,
turne our captivitee.
5 Who sow in teares, shall reape in joy.
6 Who doe goe forth,& mourne,
bearing choise seed, shall sure with joye
bringing their sheaves returne.

psalme 127.
A song of degrees for Solomon.

IF God build not the house, vainly
who build it doe take paine:
except the Lord the citty keepe,
the watchman wakes in vaine.

2 I'ts

2 I'ts vaine for you early to rife,
    watch late, to feed upon
  the bread of grief: fo hee gives fleep
  to his beloved one.

3 Loe, the wombes fruit, it's Gods reward
    fonnes are his heritage.

4 As arrows in a ftrong mans hand,
    are fons of youthfull age.

5 O bleffed is the man which hath
    his quiver fill'd with thofe:
  they fhall not be afham'd, i'th gate
    when they fpeake with their foes.

Pfalme 128.
A fong of degrees.

B Leffed is every one
  that doth Iehovah feare:
  that walks his wayes along.

2   For thou fhalt eate *with cheare*
    thy hands labour:
  bleft fhalt thou bee,
  it well with thee
    fhall be therefore.'

3   Thy wife like fruitfull vine
  fhall be by thine houfe fide:
  the children that be thine
  like olive plants abide
    about thy board.

4   Behold thus bleft
  that man doth reft,
    that feares the *Lord.*
  Iehovah fhall thee bleffe

from

from Sion, & shalt see
Ierusalems goodnes
all thy lifes dayes that bee.

6 And shalt view well
thy children then
with their children,
  peace on Isr'ell.

  Psalme 129.
  A song of degrees.

FRom my youth, now may Isr'ell say,
 oft have they mee assaild:
2 They mee assaild oft from my youth,
 yet 'gainst mee nought prevaild.
3 The ploughers plough'd upon my back,
 their furrows long they drew:
4 The righteous Lord the wickeds cords
 he did asunder-hew.
5 Let all that Sion hate be sham'd,
 and turned back together.
6 As grasse on house tops, let them be,
 which ere it's grown, doth wither:
7 Wherof that which might fill his hand
 the mower doth not finde:
nor therewith hee his bosome fills
 that doth the sheaves up binde.
8 Neither doe they that passe by, say,
 Iehovahs blessing bee
on you: you in Iehovahs Name
 a blessing with doe wee.

  Psalme 130.
  A song of degrees.
   H h

      psalme

PSALM C xxx, Cxxxi.

LORD, from the depth I cryde to thee.
  My voice Lord, doe thou heare:
unto my supplications voice
    let be attent thine eare.
2 Lord, who should stand? if thou o Lord
    sheuldst mark iniquitee.
4 But with thee there forgivenes is:
    that feared thou maist bee.
3 I for the Lord wayt, my soule wayts:
    & I hope in his word.
6 Then morning watchers watch for morn,
    more my soule for the Lord.
7 In God hope Isr'ell, for mercy
    is with the Lord: with him
8 there's much redemption. From all's sin
    hee Isr'ell will redeem.

Psalme 131.
A song of degrees, of David.

MY heart's not haughty, Lord,
  nor lofty are mine eyes:
in things too great, or high for mee,
    is not mine exercise.
2 Surely my selfe I have
    compos'd, and made to rest
like as a child that weaned is,
    from off his mothers brest:
    Im'e like a weaned child.
3 Let Israell then stay
with expectation on the Lord,
    from henceforth and for aye.

Psalme 132

A song

PSALME CxxxII.

A song of degrees.

REmember David, Lord,
and all's affliction:

2 How to the Lord he swore, & vow'd
to Iacobs mighty one.

3 Surely I will not goe
my houses tent into:
upon the pallate of my bed,
thither I will not go.

4 I will not verily
give sleep unto mine eyes:
nor will I give to mine eye-lidds
slmber *in any wise,*

5 Vntill that for the Lord
I doe finde out a seate:
a fixed habitation,
for Iacobs God so great.

6 Behould, at Epratah,
there did wee of it heare:
ev'n in the plain-fields of the wood
wee found it *to be there.*

7 Wee'l goe into his tents:
wee'l at his footstoole bow.

8 Arise, Lord, thou into thy rest:
and th'Arke of thy strength *now.*

9 Grant that thy priests may be
cloathed with righteousnes:

o let thy holy ones likewise
shout forth for joyfullnes.

10 Let not for Davids sake   *2 part.*
a servant unto thee,

Hh 2   the

the face of thine annoynted one
   away quite turned bee.

11   The Lord to David sware
   truth, nor will turne from it;
thy bodyes fruit, of them I'le make
   upon thy throne to sit.

12   If thy sons keep my law,
   and covenant, I teach them;
upon thy throne for evermore
   shall sit their children then.

13   Because Iehovah hath
   made choise of *mount* Sion:
he hath desired it to bee
   his habitation.

14   This is my resting place
   to perpetuity:
here will I dwell, and that because
   desired it have I.

15   Blesse her provision
   abundantly I will:
the poore that be in her with bread
   by mee shall have their fill.

16   Her Priests with saving health
   them also I will clad:
her holy ones likewise they shall
   with shouting loud be glad.

17   The horne of David I
   will make to bud forth there:
a candle I prepared have
   for mine annoynted *deare.*

18   His enemies I will

with

with shame apparrell them:
but flourishing upon himselfe
shall be his Diademe.

Psalme 133.

A song of degrees, of David.

HOw good and sweet o see,
i'ts for brethren to dwell
together in unitee:

2 It's like choise oyle *that fell*
the head upon,
that downe did flow
the beard unto,
 beard of Aron:
The skirts of his garment
that unto them went downe;

3 Like Hermons dews descent,
Sions mountaines upon,
 for there to bee
the Lords blessing,
life aye lasting
 commandeth hee.

Annother of the same.

HOw good it is, o see,
and how it pleaseth well,
together ev'n in unitie
for brethren soe to dwell:

2 I'ts like the choise oyntment
from head, to'th beard did go,
downe Arons beard: downeward that went
his garments skirts unto.

3 As Hermons dew, which did

Hh 2

on Sions hill defcend:
for there the Lord bleffing doth bid,
ev'n life without an end.

Pfalme 134.

A fong of degrees.

O All yee fervants of the Lord,
behold the Lord bleffe yee;
yee who within Iehovahs houfe
i'th night time ftanding bee.

2 Lift up your hands, and bleffe the Lord,
in's *place* of holines.

3. The Lord that heav'n & earth hath made,
thee out of Sion blefs.

Pfalme 135.

THe Lord praife, praife ye the Lords Name:
the Lords fervants o praife him yee.

2 That in the Lords houfe ftand: *the fame*
i'th Courts of our Gods houfe who bee.

3 The Lord prayfe, for the Lord is good:
for fweet its to his Name to fing.

4. For Iacob to him chofe hath God:
& Ifr'ell for his pretious thing.

5 For that the Lord is great I know:
& over all gods, our Lord keeps.

6 All that he wills, the Lord doth do,
in heav'n, earth, feas, & in all deeps.

7 The vapours he doth them conftraine,
forth from the ends of th'earth to rife;
he maketh lightning for the raine:
the winde brings from his treafuries.

(2)

8   Of Egipt he the first borne smit:
and that of man, of beasts also.

9   Sent wondrous signes midst thee, Egipt:
on *Pharoah*, on all's servants too.

10   Who smote great natiõs, slew great King

11   Slew Sihon King of th'Amorites,
Og also one of Bashans kings:
all kingdomes of the Cananites,

12   And gave their land an heritage:
his people Isr'ells lot to fall.

13   For aye thy Name, Lord, through each age
o Lord, is thy memoriall.

14   For his folks judge, the Lord is hee:
and of his servants he'le repent.

15   The heathens Idols silver bee,
& gold: mens hands did them invent.

16   Mouths have they, yet they never spake:
eyes have they, but they doe not see:

17   Eares have they, but no hearing take
& in their mouth no breathings bee.

18   They that them make, have their likenes:
that trust in them so is each one.

19   The Lord o house of Isr'ell bless;
the Lord blesse, thou house of Aaron,

20   O house of Levi, blesse the Lord:
who feare the Lord, blesse ye the Lord.

21   From Sion blessed be the Lord;
who dwells at Salem praise the Lord.

Psalme 136.

psalme

PSALM Cxxxvi.

O Thank the Lord, for hee is good:
  for's mercy lasts for aye.

2 Give thanks unto the God of gods:
  for's mercy is alway.

3 Give thanks unto the Lord of lords:
  for's mercy lasts for aye.

4 To him who only doth great signes:
  for's mercy is alway.

5 To him whose wisdome made the heav'ns:
  for's mercy &c.

6 Who o're the waters spread the earth:
  for's mercy &c.

7 Vnto him that did make great lights:
  for's mercy &c.

8 The Sun for ruling of the day:
  for's mercy &c.

9 The Moone and Stars to rule by night:
  for's mercy &c.

10 To him who Egipts first-borne smote:
  for's mercy &c.

11 And from amongst them Isr'ell brought:
  for's mercy &c.

12 With strong hand, & with stretcht-out arme:
  for's mercy &c.

13 To him who did the red sea part:
  for's mercy &c.

14 And through i'ts midst made Isr'ell goe:
  for's mercy &c.

15 But there drownd Pharoah & his hoast:
  for's mercy &c.

16 His people who through desart led:
                for's

for's mercy &c.

17 To him which did smite mighty Kings:
   for's mercy &c.

18 And put to slaughter famous Kings:
   for's mercy &c.

19 Sihon King of the Amorites:
   for's mercy &c.

20 And Og who was of Bashan King:
   for's mercy &c.

21 And gave their land an heritage:
   for's mercy &c.

22 A lot his servant Israell to:
   for's mercy &c.

23 In our low 'state who minded us:
   for's mercy &c.

24 And us redeemed from our foes:
   for's mercy &c.

25 Who giveth food unto all flesh:
   for's mercy lasts for ay.

26 Vnto the God of heav'n give thanks
   for's mercy is alway.

Psalme 137.

THe rivers on of Babilon
   there when wee did sit downe:
yea even then wee mourned, when
   wee remembred Sion.

2 Our Harps wee did hang it amid,
   upon the willow tree.

3 Because there they that us away
   led in captivitee,
Requir'd of us a song, & thus
        I i

                                  asks

askt mirth: us waste who laid,
sing us among a Sions song,
  unto us then they said.
4 The lords song sing can wee? being
5   in strangers land. Then let
loose her skill my right hand, if I
  Ierusalem forget..
6 Let cleave my tongue my pallate on,
  if minde thee doe not I:
if chiefe joyes or'e I prize not more
  Ierusalem my joy.
7 Remember Lord, Edoms sons word,
  unto the ground said they,
it rase, it rase, when as it was
  Ierusalem her day.
8 Blest shall hee bee, that payeth thee,
  daughter of Babilon,
who must be waste: that which thou hast
  rewarded us upon.
9 O happie hee shall surely bee
  that taketh up, that eke
thy little ones against the stones
  doth into pieces breake.

Psalme 138.
A psalme of David.

VVIthall my heart, I'le prayse thee now:
  before the gods I'le sing to thee.
2 Toward thine holy Temple bow,
  & praise thy Name for thy mercee,
    & thy truth: for thy word thou hye
or'e all thy Name dost magnify.

3 I'th

PSALME Cxxxviii.

3   It'h day I cride, thou anfwredft meet,
with ftrength thou didft my foule up-beare.

4   Lord, all the earths kings fhall praife thee,
the word when of thy mouth they heare.

5   Yea, they fhall fing in the Lords wayes,
for great's Iehovahs glorious prayfe.

6   Albeit that the Lord be hye,
refpect yet hath he to the low:
but as for them that are lofty,
he them doth at a diftance know.

7   Though in the midft I walking bee
of trouble thou wilt quicken mee,
Forth fhalt thou make thine hand to go
againft their wrath that doe me hate;
thy right hand fhall me fave alfo.

8   The Lord will perfect mine eftate:
thy mercy Lord, for ever ftands:
leave not the works of thine owne hands.

Another of the fame.

VVIthall my heart, I'le thee confefs:
thee praife the gods before.

2 The Temple of thine holines
towards it I'le adore:
Alfo I will confeffe thy Name,
for thy truth, & mercy:
becaufe thou over all thy Name
thy word doft magnify.

3 In that fame day that I did cry,
thou didft mee anfwer make:
thou ftrengthnedft mee with ftrength, which I
within my foule *did take.*

Ii 2

4 O

4 O Lord, when thy mouths words they heare
    all earths Kings shall thee praise.
5 And for the Lords great glory, there
    they shall sing in his wayes.
6 Albeit that the Lord be high,
    yet hee respects the low:
but as for them that are lofty
    hee them far off doth know.
7 Though I in midst of trouble go,
    thee quickning mee I haue:
thy hand thou wilt cast on my foe,
    thy right hand shall mee saue.
8 The Lord will perfect it for mee:
    thy mercy ever stands,
Lord, doe not those forsake that bee
    the works of thine owne hands.

Psalme 139.
To the chief musician, a psalme
of David.

O LORD, thou hast me searcht & knowne.
    Thou knowst my sitting downe,
&c mine up-rising: my thought is
    to thee afarre off knowne.
2 Thou knowst my paths, & lying downe,
    & all my wayes knowst well.
4 For loe, each word that's in my tongue,
    Lord, thou canst fully tell.
3 Behinde thou gird'st mee, & before:
    & layst on mee thine hand.
6 Such knowledge is too strange, too high,
    for mee to understand

                      7 where

7 Where shall I from thy presence go?
  or where from thy face flye?
8 If heav'n I climbe, thou there, loe thou,
  if downe in hell I lye.
9 If I take mornings wings; & dwell
  where utmost sea-coasts bee.
10 Ev'n there thy hand shall mee conduct:
  & thy right hand hold mee.
11 That veryly the darknes shall
  mee cover, if I say:
  then shall the night about mee be
  like to the lightsome day.
12 Yea, darknes hideth not from thee,
  but as the day shines night:
  alike unto thee both these are,
  the darknes & the light.
13 Because that thou possessed hast
  my reines: and covered mee
  within my mothers wombe thou hast.
14 My prayse shall be of thee,
  Because that I am fashioned
  in fearfull wondrous wise:
  & that thy works are merveilous,
  my soule right well descries.
          (2)
15 From thee my substance was not hid,
  when made I was closely:
  & when within th'earths lowest parts
  I was wrought curiously.
16 Thine eyes upon my substance yet
  imperfected, did look,
          Ii 3
                                    and

& all the members that I have
were written in thy booke,
What dayes they ſhould be faſhioned:
none of them yet were come.

17 How pretious are thy thoughts to mee,
o God? how great's their ſumme?

18 If I ſhould count them, in number.
more then the ſands they bee:
& at whatime I doe awake,
ſtill I abide with thee.

19 Aſſuredly thou wilt o God,
thoſe that be wicked ſlay:
yee that are bloody men, therefore
depart from mee away.

20 Becauſe that they againſt thee doe
ſpeake wickedly *likewiſe*:
thy Name they doe take up in vaine
who are thine enemies.

21 Thy haters Lord, doe I not hate?
& am not I with thoſe
offended grievouſly that doe
up-riſing thee oppoſe?

22 Them I with perfect hatred hate
I count them as my foes.

23 Search mee o God, & know my heart:
try mee, my thoughts diſcloſe:

24 And ſee if any wicked way
in mee there bee at all:
& mee conduct within the way
that laſt for ever ſhall.

Palme 140

pſalm

PSALME CxL

To the chief muſician, a pſalme
of David,

LORD, free mee from the evill man:
from violent man ſave mee.
2 Whoſe hearts thinke miſchief: every day
for war they gathred bee.
3 Their tongues they have made to be ſharp
a ſerpent like unto:
the poyſon of the Aſpe it is
under their lipps *alſo.*   Selah.
4 Keepe mee, Lord, from the wickeds hands,
from violent man mee ſave:
my goings who to overthrow
in thought projected have.
5 The proud have hid a ſnare for mee,
cords alſo: they a net
have ſpred abroad by the way ſide:
grins for mee they have ſet.   Selah
6 Vnto Iehovah I did ſay,
thou art a God to mee:
Lord heare the voice of my requeſts,
which are for grace to thee.

(2)

7 O God, the Lord, who art the ſtay
of my ſalvation:
my head by thee hath covered been
the day of battell on.
8 Thoſe mens deſires that wicked are
Iehovah, doe not grant,
their wicked purpoſe furher nor,
leſt they themſelves doe vaunt.

9 As

9 As for the head of them that mee
    doe round about inclose,
  o let the molestation
    of their lips cover those.
10 Let burning coales upon them fall,
    into the fire *likewise*
  let them be cast, into deepe pits,
    that they no more may rise.
11 Let not i'th earth establisht bee
    men of an evill tongue:
  evill shall hunt to overthrow
    the man of violent wrong.
12 The afflicteds cause, the poore mans right,
    I know God will maintaine:
13 Yea, just shall praise thy Name: th'upright
  shall 'fore thy face remaine.

Psalme 141.
A psalme of David.

O GOD, my Lord, on thee I call,
    doe thou make hast to mee:
and harken thou unto my voice,
    when I cry unto thee.
2 And let my pray'r directed be
    as incense in thy sight:
and the up-lifting of my hands
    as sacrifice at night.
3 Iehovah: oh that thou would'st set
    a watch my mouth before:
as also of my lips with care
    o doe thou keepe the dore.
4 Bow not my heart to evill things;

to

PSALME Cxlr,

to doe the wicked deed
with wicked workers: & let not
mee of their dainties feed.

5 Let just men smite mee, kindenes 'tis;
let him reprove mee eke,
it shall be such a pretious oyle,
my head it shall not breake:
For yet my prayr's ev'n in their woes.

6   When their judges are cast
on rocks, then shall they heare my words,
for they are sweet to taste.

7 Like unto one who on the earth
doth cutt & cleave the wood,
ev'n so our bones at the graves mouth
are scattered abroad.

8 But unto thee o God, the Lord
directed are mine eyes:
my soule o leave not destitute,
on thee my hope relyes.

9 O doe thou keepe mee from the snare
which they have layd for mee;
& also from the grins of those
that work iniquitee.

10 Together into their owne nets
o let the wicked fall:
untill such time that I escape
may make from them withall.

Psalme 142.

Maschil of David, a prayer when
he was in the cave.

K k

psalm

PSALM Cxlii.

VNto Iehovah with my voice,
 I did unto him cry:
unto Iehovah with my voice
 my sute for grace made I.

2 I did poure out before his face
 my meditation:
before his face I did declare
 the trouble mee upon.

3 O'rewhelm'd in mee when was my spirit,
 then thou didst know my way:
I'th way I walkt, a snare for mee
 they privily did lay.

4 On my right hand I lookt, & saw,
 but no man would mee know,
all refuge faild mee: for my soule
 none any care did show.

5 Then to thee Lord, I cryde, & sayd,
 my hope thou art *alone*:
& in the land of living ones
 thou art my portion.

6 Because I am brought very low,
 attend unto my cry:
from my pursuers save thou mee,
 which stronger bee then I.

7 That I thy Name may praise, my soule
 from prison oh bring out:
when thou shalt mee reward, the just
 shall compasse mee about.

Psalme 143.
A psalme of David.

psalm

266

PSALME Cxliii.

LORD, heare my prayr, give eare when I
doe supplicate to thee:
in thy truth, in thy righteousnes;
make answer unto mee.

2 And into judgement enter not
with him that serveth thee;
for in thy sight no man that lives
can justified bee.

3 For th'enemie hath pursude my soule,
my life to'th ground hath throwne:
& made mee dwell i'th dark like them
that dead are long agone.

4 Therefore my spirit is overwhelmd
perplexedly in mee:
my heart also within mee is
made desolate to bee.

5 I call to minde the dayes of old,
I meditation use
on all thy words: upon the work
of thy hands I doe muse.

6 I even I doe unto thee
reach mine out-stretched hands;
so after thee my soule doth thirst
as doe the thristy lands.   Selah.

(2)

7 Hast, Lord, heare mee, my spirit doth faile,
hide not thy face mee fro:
lest I become like one of them
that downe to pit doe go.

8 Let mee thy mercy heare i'th morne,
for I doe on thee stay,

Kk 2   wherin

wherin that I should walk cause mee
to understand the way:
For unto thee I lift my soule.

9   O Lord deliver mee
from all mine enemies; I doe flye
to hide my selfe with thee.

10 Because thou art my God, thy will
oh teach thou mee to doe,
thy spirit is good: of uprightnes
lead mee the land into.

11 Iehovah, mee o quicken thou
ev'n for thine owne Names sake;
And for thy righteousnes my soule
from out of trouble take.

12 Doe thou also mine enemies
cut off in thy mercy,
destroy them that afflict my soule:
for thy servant am I.

Psalme 144.

A psalme of David.

O Let Iehovah blessed be
who is my rock of might,
who doth instruct my hands to war,
and my fingers to fight.

2 My goodnes, fortresse, my hye towre,
& that doth set mee free:
my shield, my trust, which doth subdue
my people under mee.

3 Iehovah, what is man, that thou
knowledge of him dost take?
what is the son of man, that thou

acount

account of him doſt make?

4 Man's like to vanity: hîs dayes
   paſſe like a ſhade away.

5 Lord, bow the heav'ns, come downe & touch
   the mounts & ſmoake ſhall they.

6 Lightning caſt forth, & ſcatter them:
   thine arrows ſhoot, them rout,

7 Thine hand o ſend thou from above,
   doe thou redeeme mee out:
   And rid mee from the waters great:
   from hand of ſtrangers brood:

8 Whoſe mouth ſpeaks lyes, their right hand is
   a right hand of falſehood.

(2)

9 O God, new ſongs I'le ſing to thee:
   upon the Pſaltery,
   and on ten ſtringed inſtrument
   to thee ſing praiſe will I.

10 It's hee that giveth unto Kings
   ſafety victorious:
   his ſervant David he doth ſave
   from ſword pernitious.

11 Rid mee from hand of ſtrange children,
   whoſe mouth ſpeakes vanity:
   & their right hand a right hand is
   of lying falſity:

12 That like as plants which are growne up
   in youth may be our ſons;
   our daughters pallace like may be
   polliſht as corner ſtones:

13 Our garners full, affording ſtore

Kk 3

of every fort of meates;
our cattell bringing thoufands forth,
  ten thoufands in our ftreets:
14 Strong let our oxen bee to work.
  that breaking in none bee
nor going out: that fo our ftreets.
  may from complaints bee free.
15 O blefled fhall the people be
  whofe ftate is fuch as this:
o blefled fhall the people be,
  whofe God Iehovah is.

Pfalme 145.

Davids pfalme of praife.

MY God, o King, I'le thee extoll
  & blefle thy Name for aye.
2 For ever will I praife thy Name;
  and blefle thee every day.
3 Great is the Lord, moft worthy praife.
  his greatnes fearch can none.
4 Age unto age fhall praife thy works:
  & thy great acts make knowne.
5 I of thy glorious honour will
  fpeake ofthy majefty;
& of the operations
  by thee done wondroufly.
6 Alfo men of thy mighty works
  fhall fpeake which dreadfull are:
alfo concerning thy greatnes,
  it I will forth declare:
7 Thy great goodnefles memory
  they largely fhall exprefs:

and

PSALME Cxlv.

and they shall with a shouting voice
sing of thy righteousnes.

8 The Lord is gracious, & hee is
full of compassion:
slow unto anger, & full of
commiseration.

9 The Lord is good to all: or'e all *part (*
his works his mercies bee.

10 All thy works shall praise thee, o Lord:
& thy Saints shall blesse thee,

11 They'le of thy kingdomes glory speake:
and talk of thy powre *bye*;

12 To make mens sons his great acts know:
his kingdomes majesty.

13 Thy Kingdome is a kingdome aye:
& thy reigne lasts alwayes.

14 The Lord doth hold up all that fall:
and all downe-bow'd ones rayse.

15 All eyes wayt on thee, & their meat
thou dost in season bring.

16 Oputst thy hand, & the desire
fil'st of each living thing.

17 In all his wayes the Lord is just:
& holy in's works all.

18 Hee's neere to all that call on him:
in truth that on him call.

19 Hee satisfy will the desire
of those that doe him feare:
Hee will be safety unto them,
and when they cry he'le beare.

20 The Lord preserves each one of them

that

that *lovers of* him bee:
but whofoever wicked are
aboliſh them doth bee.
21 My mouth the prayſes of the Lord
by ſpeaking ſhall expreſs:
alſo all fleſh his holy Name
for evermore ſhall bleſs.

Pſalme 146.

THe Lord praiſe: praiſe(my ſoule)the Lord.
So long as I doe live
I'le praiſe the Lord; while that I am,
praiſe to my God I'le give.
3 Truſt not in Princes; nor mans ſon
who can no ſuccour ſend.
4 His breath goe's forth,to's earth he turnes,
his thoughts that day doe end.
5 Happie is hee that hath the God
of Iacob for his ayd:
whoſe expectation is upon
Iehovah his God ſtayd
6 Which heav'n,earth,ſea,all in them made:
truth keeps for evermore:
7 Which for th'oppreſſed judgement doth,
gives to the hungry ſtore,
8 The Lord doth looſe the priſoners.
the Lord ope's eyes of blinde,
the Lord doth raiſe the bowed downe;
the Lord to'th juſt is kinde.
9 The Lord ſaves ſtangers, & relievs
the orphan & widow:
but hee of them that wicked are

the

the way doth overthrow.

10 The Lord ſhall reigne for evermore,
thy God, o Sion, hee
to generations all ſhall reigne:
o prayſe Iehovah yee.

Pſalme 147.

PRayſe yee the Lord, for it
is good praiſes to ſing,
to our God for it's ſweet,
praiſe is a comely thing.

2   Ieruſalem
the Lord up-reares,
outcaſts gathers
of Iſrë'll *them.*

3 The broke in heart he heales:
& up their wounds doth binde.

4 The ſtars by number tells:
hee calls them all by kinde.

5   Our Lord great is,
& of great might,
yea infinite
his knowledge 'tis.

6 The Lord ſets up the low:
wicked to ground doth fling.

7 Sing thanks the Lord unto
on Harp, our Gods praiſe ſing.

8   Who clouds the ſkyes,
to earth gives raines:
who on mountaines
makes graſſe to riſe.

9 Beaſts, hee & ravens young

L l

when

when as they cry feeds then.

10 Ioyes not in horſes ſtrong:
nor in the leggs of men.

11   The Lord doth place
his pleaſure where
men doe him feare,
    & hope on's grace.

12 Ieruſalem, God praiſe:
Sion thy God conteſs:

13 For thy gates barres he ſtayes:
in thee thy ſons doth bleſs.

14   Peace maketh hee
in borders thine:
with wheat ſo fine
    hee filleth thee.

15 On earth ſends his decree:
ſwiftly his word doth paſs.

16 Gives ſnow like wool, ſpreds hee
his hoare froſt aſhes as.

17   His yce doth caſt
like morſels to:
'fore his cold who
    can ſtand ſtedfaſt?

18 His word ſends, & them thaws:
makes winde blow, water flows.

19 His word, Iacob; his laws,
& judgements Iſr'ell ſhows.

20   Hee hath ſo done
no nation to,
judgements alſo
    they have not knowne.
      Hallelujah,

pſalme

PSALME Cxlviii.

Pſalme 148. Hallelujah.

FRom heav'n o praiſe the Lord:
   him praiſe the heights within.

2 All's Angells praiſe afford,
   all's Armies praiſe yee him.

3   O give him praiſe
  Sun & Moone *bright*:
  all Stars of light,
    o give him praiſe.

4 Yee heav'ns of heav'ns him praiſe:
  or'e heav'ns yee waters *cleare*.

5 The Lords Name let them praiſe:
  for hee ſpake, made they were.

6   Them ſtabliſht hee
  for ever & aye:
  nor ſhall away
    his made decree.

7 Praiſe God from tn'earth *below*:
  yee dragons & each deepe.

8 Fire & haile, miſt & ſnow:
  whirl-windes his word which keepe.

9   Mountaines, alſo
  you hills all yee:
  each fruitfull tree,
    all Cedars too.

10 Beaſts alſo all cattell:
  things creeping, foules that flye.

11 Earths kings, & all people:
  princes, earths judges *bye*:
    doe all the ſame.

12 Young men & maids:

Ll 2

old

275

old men & babes.

13   Praiſe the Lords Name,
For his Name's hye only:
his glory o're earth & heav'n.

14 His folks horne he lifts hye
the praiſe of all's Saints, ev'n
the ſons who bee
of Iſraell,
his neere people,
the Lord praiſe yee.

Pſalme **149.**

PRaiſe yee the Lord: unto the Lord
doe yee ſing a new ſong:
& in the congregation
his praiſe the Saints among.

2 Let Iſraell now joyfull bee
in him who him hath made:
children of Sion in their King
o let them be full glad.

3 O let them with *melodious* flute
his Name give praiſe unto:
let them ſing praiſes unto him
with Timbrell, Harp alſo.

4 Becauſe Iehovah in his folk
doth pleaſure greatly take;
the meek hee with ſalvation
ev'n beautifull will make.

5 Let them the gracious Saints that be
moſt gloriouſly rejoyce:
& as they lye upon their beds
lift up their ſinging voyce.

6 let

6 Let their mouths have Gods praise: their hand
  a two edg'd sword also:
7 On heathen vengeance, on the folk
  punishment for to do:
8 Their kings with chaines, with yron bolts
  also their peers to binde:
9 To doe on them the judgement writ:
  all's Saints this honour finde.
                    Hallelujah.

Psalme 150.

PRaise yee the Lord, praise God
  in's place of holines:
O praise him in the firmament
  of his great mightines.
2 O praise him for his acts
   that be magnificent:
& praise yee him according to
  his greatnes excellent.
3 With Trumpet praise yee him
   that gives a sound so hye:
& doe yee praise him with the Harp,
  & sounding Psalterye.
4 With Timbrell & with Flute
   praise unto him give yee:
with Organs, & string'd instruments
  prais'd by you let him bee.
5 Vpon the loude Cymballs
   unto him give yee praise:
upon the Cimballs praise yee him
  which hye their sound doe raise,

                    Ll 3

                                        6 Let

PSALM CI.

6   Let every thing to which
the Lord doth breath afford
the praifes of the Lord fet forth:
o doe yee praife the Lord.

FINIS.

An admonition to the Reader.

THe verfes of thefe pfalmes may be reduced to
fix kindes, the firft wherof may be fung in very neere fourty common tunes; as they are collected, out of our chief muficians, by *Tho. Ravenf-
croft.*

The fecond kinde may be fung in three tunes as
Pf. 25. 50. & 67. in our englifh pfalm books.

The third. may be fung indifferently, as *pf.* the 51.
100. & ten cōmandements, in our englifh pfalme
books. which three tunes aforefaid, comprehend
almoft all this whole book of pfalmes, as being
tunes moft familiar to us.

The fourth. as *pf.* 148. of which there are but a-
bout five.

The fift. as *pf.* 112. or the *Pater nofter*, of which
there are but two. *viz.* 85. & 138.

The fixt. as *pf.* 113. of which but one, *viz.* 115.

Faults escaped in printing.

Escaped.	Right
pfalme 9. vers 9. opreſt.	oppreſt.
v. 10. knowes.	know.
pſ. 18. u. 29. the.	thee.
u. 31. 3 part wanting.	3 part.
pſ. 19. u. 13, let thou-	kept back
kept back.	o let:
pſ. 21 u. 8. the Lord.	thine hand.
pſ. 145 u. 6. Feuen I.	moreover I.

The reſt, which have eſcaped through over-
fight, you may amend, as you finde
them obvious.

CPSIA information can be obtained
at www.ICGtesting.com
Printed in the USA
BVOW09s2043310517
485651BV00003B/229/P